Yours ever truly
James Croll

AUTOBIOGRAPHICAL
SKETCH

OF

JAMES CROLL

LL.D., F.R.S., ETC.

WITH

Memoir of his Life and Work

BY

JAMES CAMPBELL IRONS, M.A.

LONDON: EDWARD STANFORD

26 AND 27 COCKSPUR STREET, CHARING CROSS, S.W.

1896

PREFACE

HAVING been one of the intimate friends who urged Dr. Croll to write an autobiographical account of his remarkable career, it fell to me to arrange the materials which he left for publication. Unfortunately, the autobiographical sketch was never completed, and together with the additional papers which came into my hands, it hardly furnished an adequate account of his life and scientific achievements. Accordingly, an effort was made to obtain further information, and various friends were asked to forward letters illustrating the development of his researches. The cordial response of several leading scientists made my task less difficult, but the time occupied in procuring and examining these materials partly accounts for the delay in the appearance of this volume.

While the work was in progress, kindly advice was given by Professor Masson regarding the Autobiography, which I cordially acknowledge. He wrote that "it is so characteristic, that it would be best to preserve it entire, as it would be a pity to lose anything of the simple and pleasant peculiarities of the autobiographical original." This course has been followed, and a more detailed account of his life and scientific work has been added. Such an arrangement involved a certain amount of overlapping and reduplication, which was hardly avoidable under the circumstances.

To many friends of Dr. Croll who forwarded letters, I beg to express my sincere thanks. In particular to Mr. Francis Darwin, who kindly gave permission to use the correspondence with his father, Mr. Charles Darwin, and to Professor G. H. Darwin, who extended a similar courtesy; to Mr. A. R. Wallace, Sir. J. D. Hooker, Professor Foster, Professor Tyndall, Rev. O. Fisher, Mrs. Romanes, Mrs. Tyndall, and many others. I have also to thank Mr. Horne and Mr. Bennie of the Geological Survey for letters, papers, and various suggestions. I beg also to acknowledge my great obligations to Mr. Herbertson, F.R.S.E., Lecturer at the Heriot - Watt College, Edinburgh, for his valuable assistance in making a digest of Dr. Croll's papers; to Mr. Fowler of the Kensington Museum for permission to use his review of the work on *Stellar Evolution*, and to Mr. Whittaker for the republication of his review of *The Philosophical Basis of Evolution*. My special thanks are likewise due to Lord Kelvin and Messrs. Macmillan & Co. for their permission to use the Obituary Notices at the end of the volume.

My brother, the Rev. David E. Irons, B.D., Glasgow, has written part of the biographical account, has aided me generally in the compilation of the work, and has revised the proof-sheets.

This volume has been written with the hope that the life of Dr. Croll, recording the triumph over his early struggles, his scientific researches, which secured him a world-wide reputation as an original thinker, and his earnest belief in the Christian faith, may prove interesting. It may only be added that the entire proceeds of its sale will be handed to his widow.

J. C. I.

10 ROYAL TERRACE, EDINBURGH,
November 1896.

PREFATORY NOTE

I HAVE been frequently urged during the past few years to draw up a statement of the principal incidents of my life. As this is a thing to which I have a strong aversion, I have hitherto declined. Induced mainly by the desire of my wife, I have at last agreed to comply with the wishes of my friends. Mrs. Croll will hurriedly jot down in pencil, to dictation, the facts as they occur to my mind. These jottings will probably never be revised or read over by me. Owing to the state of my head, and the pressure of work of a more important character, I am obliged to adopt this course. Besides, it is a sort of work to which I am naturally ill adapted, being almost devoid of the faculty for descriptive writing.

J. C.

PERTH, *December 7,* 1887.

CONTENTS

LIFE OF JAMES CROLL

——◆——

AUTOBIOGRAPHICAL SKETCH

MY ancestors, who spelled their name Croil, and some of them, it would seem, Croyl, were inhabitants of the parish of Cargill for at least more than the last two centuries; for I have been able, from the parish baptismal register, to trace my direct parentage back till about the middle of the seventeenth century, that is, as far back as the register extends.

I was born at Little Whitefield, parish of Cargill, on Tuesday, January 2, 1821, at eleven o'clock P.M. It was a cold wintry night, with the snow lying thickly on the ground. I was the second of a family of four sons. My father David Croil, son of Alexander Croil, was born in March 1781, and was consequently forty years of age when I was born. He was a stonemason by trade. Little Whitefield, now a farmhouse, was then a small village of some eight or ten houses. Beside the village were a hundred or a hundred and fifty acres of land, divided principally amongst four of the villagers: namely, William Brewster, James Brown, William Marshall (I think), and my father. The village was demolished, and the land put into one farm, when I was about three years of age.

My forefathers had resided at that village for several generations past. My mother, Janet Ellis, youngest daughter of James Ellis, was born at Elgin in 1781, and was consequently of the same age as my father. She left Morayshire for Perth during the earlier part of the present century, and was married to my father, some time, I think, about the latter end of 1818. Both my parents possessed a considerable amount of individuality of character. Mentally, however, they were considerably diverse. My mother was firm, shrewd, and observing, and gifted with a considerable amount of what is called in Scotland "common sense." My father was mild, thoughtful, and meditative, and possessed of strong religious and moral sentiments. This amiable disposition and high moral character made him greatly esteemed and respected. But he had the misfortune to possess a most anxious and sensitive mind. I was supposed to possess a considerable share of the peculiarities of both parents, with, no doubt, a predominance of those of my father. I have often thought that, had I possessed some more of my mother's qualities, and less of some of my father's, the battle of life would not have proved so painful to me. When a boy, I was always proud to tell, when asked, who my father was; for the mention of his name generally commanded respect, and procured for me a kindly word, with the remark, " I hope that when you grow up you will be as good a man as your father."

As already stated, I was the second of a family of four sons. Alexander, the eldest, was born on November 29, 1819, and died when about ten years of age. His death was a severe blow to my parents, especially to my father, who never afterwards regained his former vivacity of spirits. My youngest brother, William, born February 25, 1826, died in infancy. David, born April 23, 1822, to whom I shall subsequently have occasion to refer, died on February 28, 1876. He had the misfortune to be deformed. He was very much hunchbacked, which was supposed to have been the result of a fall from a servant's arms, when he was an infant.

When the proprietor of the parish, or, at least, of the greater part of it, the Right Honourable Lord Willoughby, decided to convert the small holdings into large farms, he allotted two pieces of ground for feuing purposes: one piece, about a mile to the south-west of Little Whitefield, now called Wolfhill; the other three miles to the north, now called Burreltown. My father took one or two feus in the former place, on which he erected a dwelling-house, and removed to it about the year 1824, when I was about three years of age.

There is very little in my infant years to which I need refer, except, it may be, to my somewhat early developed power of memory. I have a most distinct remembrance of witnessing the ceremony of my brother David's baptism. My father being a Congregationalist, and a member of the Rev. William Orme's church in Perth, that minister came out and preached an out-door sermon to the villagers on the occasion of the baptism; and I have a vivid remembrance of the scene, although I could not then have been over eighteen months old. I have also a remembrance of a number of little incidents which occurred before I was three years of age, among which was the flitting-day from Little Whitefield to Wolfhill. After this date there are very few long breaks in my remembrance. I suppose I must have inherited this faculty from my father, who told me that he had a distinct remembrance of things which occurred when he was only two years old.

For the first three or four years after removing to Wolfhill nothing of importance occurred worth recording. I was not early sent to school, my parents having been, as I think, judiciously opposed to too early mental work. Another cause was that, about this time, I became afflicted with a rather troublesome pain on the top or about the opening of the head, which prevented me being able, except in the heat of summer, to remain bareheaded; and, as I could not be persuaded to sit in school with my cap on, my parents had for a considerable time to allow me to remain at home. My first lessons were consequently obtained from my parents, assisted by my eldest brother. The village schoolmaster also now and again gave me private lessons at home. In this way I learned to read and write. The village school to which I refer was a very poor affair indeed. An elderly man, who had seen better days, taught, for a living, a few boys in a private house. A year or two afterwards I went, for a short time, to the parish school, a mile and a half distant from Wolfhill; and subsequently I attended a Voluntary school at Guildtown two miles to the west of the village. The teacher there was rather harsh and tyrannical; and the consequence was that I abhorred school, and, as might be expected, made very little progress. Next year, however, 1834, he was succeeded by a Mr. Keiller, a man of more genial nature. I remained with him some eight or nine months, and then had to leave school finally. The cause of my having to leave so soon was this. My father, having one or two acres of ground, kept a cow, and as he was away from home during the greater part of the year, following his duties as a stonemason, I had to be taken from school to assist my mother at home.

I must say that I was rather a dull scholar, scarcely up to the average of boys of the same age, as far as regards getting up my lessons sharply and correctly. I never succeeded in acquiring an accurate style of reading, and by no amount of labour could I manage to become even a moderately good speller. I unfortunately left school just at the time I was beginning to have a longing desire for a much better education. The circumstances which led to this desire I shall now narrate.

Up to the years of eleven or so I had little or no love for reading; being much fonder of play than of books. This somewhat disappointed my father. One day during the summer of 1832, when at Perth, I observed in a bookseller's window the first number of the *Penny Magazine*, which had just appeared. Attracted by the illustrations, I went in and purchased it. This incident led to a new epoch in my life. Having read the first number with interest, I then purchased the second, third, and succeeding numbers as they appeared, all of which I read with zest. Shortly after I had commenced to read the *Penny Magazine*, a book on natural philosophy, Dick's *Christian Philosopher*, I think, or some other of his books, came under my notice. Commencing to read it, I was at once struck with the novelty of the ideas. I shortly afterwards procured one or two other books on physical science, among which was Joyce's famous scientific dialogues. At first I became bewildered, but soon the beauty and simplicity of the conceptions filled me with delight and astonishment, and I began then in earnest to study the matter. I may here mention that, even at the very commencement of my studies, it was not the facts and details of the physical sciences which riveted my attention, but the laws or principles which they were intended to illustrate. This necessarily determined me to study the sciences in something like systematic form; for, in order to understand a given law, I was generally obliged to make myself acquainted with the preceding law or conditions on which it depended. I remember well that, before I could make headway in physical astronomy (and this was the only branch of astronomy which I have ever studied), I had to go back and study the laws of motion and the fundamental principles of mechanics. In like manner I studied pneumatics, hydrostatics, light, heat, electricity, and magnetism. I obtained assistance from no one. In fact, there were none of my acquaintances who knew anything whatever about these subjects. Notwithstanding all these disadvantages under which I laboured, I managed in the course of four years or so, or by the time I was between fifteen and sixteen years old, to obtain a pretty tolerable knowledge of all the general principles of those branches of physical science. The reason of my being enabled at this early age to make so much progress in so short a time was, as I have already stated, that it was the principles or laws to which my attention was mainly, if not exclusively directed. In studying, for example, the electrical machine or the air-pump, I paid little or no attention to the details of their various parts, further than as they illustrated the electrical or the pneumatic laws according to which these machines operated. The consequence was that these multifarious details soon disappeared from the memory, and the laws or principles only remained.

There were two important and, to most people, interesting sciences for which I had no relish, namely, chemistry and geology, more particularly the latter. The reason was that to me they appeared so full of details and so deficient in rational principles, being so much sciences of observation and experiment. Had any one told me then that one day I should be a professional geologist, I would have regarded the statement as incredible. In truth, it was more by accident than by choice that I became a geologist. Geology is almost the only science on which (with the exception of one department of it, to which I shall afterwards have occasion to refer) I have never spent a single day's earnest study. However, the accident of becoming a member of the Geological Survey was of immense advantage to me when I afterwards became engaged in my climatological studies; for it enabled me to become acquainted with geological phenomena necessary for the subject, of which otherwise I would have remained ignorant, and without which my work would have been but very imperfectly accomplished.

No grand physical conceptions acquired in after years ever made such an impression on my mind as those of this early date, except it be those relating to the modern science of energy, which was not then in existence; namely, the transformation and conservation of energy, and the dynamical theory and mechanical equivalent of heat. My early acquaintance with the general principles of physical science has been of great service to me in after years.

In the summer of 1837, when I was between sixteen and seventeen years of age, the question arose—what occupation or handicraft was I to follow? This was a point somewhat difficult to determine; for I had no liking for any particular occupation, nor was it supposed that I possessed any special fitness for one occupation more than another. The bent of my mind at the time was to obtain a university education, which might enable me to follow out physical science. This, however, was a wish that could not be realised, as my father was by far too poor. After several days' consideration I thought I might try the occupation of a millwright. As I was fond of theoretical mechanics, it occurred to me that this occupation might be the most congenial and the one for which I was best adapted. But this I afterwards found to be a mistake; for, although I was familiar with theoretical mechanics, yet, as a working mechanic, I was scarcely up to the average. The strong natural tendency of my mind toward abstract thinking somehow unsuited me for the practical details of daily work.

After it was decided that I was to be a millwright, I was engaged as an apprentice to a millwright at Collace, a village at the foot of Dunsinane Hill, three miles distant from home. In 1841, at the termination of my engagement, I left Collace, and worked for two years as a journeyman with a firm of the name of Martin & Robertson, Banchory, near Coupar-Angus. The wages received were small, being only eight shillings a week, with food, which was of the poorest description possible. As my employers were in difficulties, small as my wages were, I lost money by them. It was on the whole rather a rough life. A very considerable part of our work consisted in the repairing of corn- saw- and thresh-ing-mills. The consequence was that we were very frequently away from home, and seldom more than a day or two at one place. During the last two years I occupied, on an average, three different beds in a week; and these were not of the most comfortable character. We millwrights had generally to go to the ploughman's bothy; and when there was no room there, we had to go to the barn or the stable loft above the horses. Frequently we had to bury ourselves under the clothes to secure protection from the rats. Having spent some five or six years as a millwright, I got tired of the trade, and resolved to try something else. I came home to Wolf-hill,—being at the time about twenty-two years of age,—and went to St. Martin's parish school for a winter to study algebra. Then, being pretty well up to woodwork, I got employment as a house joiner in the beginning of summer. After a little practice, I soon found this a far more congenial occupation. The first job, in the joiner way, in which I was engaged, was at the Free Church which was being erected at Kinrossie, parish of Collace, for the Rev., now Dr., Andrew A. Bonar. After the church was finished, work became scarce in the neighbourhood, and, in the summer of 1844, I went to Glasgow in search of employment. There I found work at once, and remained for a few months, afterwards removing to Paisley, where I remained for upwards of a year. I liked both the place and my employment. But my stay here was brought to a sudden termination in the spring of 1846, in the twenty-fifth year of my age, by an event which had the effect of changing the whole course of my future life. When a boy of about ten or eleven years of age, I had what is called a boil on my left elbow joint. One day it was accidentally knocked against the corner of a door, and this had the effect of preventing it healing up. It, however, proved of very little inconvenience to me, except that now and again, especially during the spring months, the elbow became somewhat inflamed. But in Paisley, at the time to which I refer, the state of the elbow began to assume a somewhat serious character, and my medical advisers informed me that it would be absolutely necessary for me to abandon my occupation as a joiner and try some easier pursuit. I accordingly took their advice, left the place, and returned home to think over what should be done.

This I felt to be a great blow to my future prospects. But although, as we shall see, it led to years of poverty and hardship, nevertheless, being freed from the long hours of manual labour, I enjoyed a great deal of leisure for reading and study. Strange are the ways of Providence. Had it not been for a mere accident in early life, I should in all likelihood have remained a working joiner till the end of my days. Here, however, before proceeding further with my narrative, I must turn back a little, in order to refer to another circumstance which exercised a very considerable influence on my future life.

Although brought up under religious influences (my parents being Independents of the good old Congregational type, having in the early part of the century joined that body), I was nevertheless, till over the age of seventeen, indifferent to divine things. During the autumn of 1839 I became deeply impressed, mainly by the reading of Boston's *Fourfold State*; and in this condition I remained for some time, till I was led to see that salvation was entirely of free grace. Simple trust in Christ's vicarious death gave me complete peace of mind and true happiness, a peace which the world can neither give nor take away. The agnostic will smile at my experience. How different would he feel if he experienced this blessed peace himself !

> " The love of Jesus, what it is
> None but His loved ones know."

Shortly afterwards a remarkable religious movement took place in the parish of Collace, where I was then residing, under the ministry of the Rev. Andrew Bonar. I was soon then amongst kindred spirits; and the year that followed was probably the happiest in my life.

Living in a retired country place, after the toils of the day, when the shadows of evening were falling, I generally took a stroll in the fields, or along a quiet road for an hour or two, to meditate and ponder over spiritual things. These hours I enjoyed exceedingly, and I continued the practice for years afterwards, until I went to reside in the city. Nothing in city life did I miss so much as these quiet walks.

> " The calm retreat, the silent shade,
> With prayer and praise agree,
> And seem by Thy sweet bounty made
> For those who follow Thee."

Almost from boyhood I had a love for retired, solitary walks in the country. On these occasions I can enjoy a congenial companion, but I would rather be alone to meditate. It is more sweet, more pleasant. The stillness of nature adds to the charm. I well remember one of the solitary musings of my early days, when I could have been only about twelve or thirteen years of age. It was this. I asked myself, What would there be, if there were no world ? The ready answer, of course, was that there would be the sun, moon, and stars. What would there be, if there were no sun, moon, and stars ? There would be God. But what would there be if there were no God ? There would be nothing but empty space. But if there were no space, what would remain ? This question staggered me. I could not in thought get quit of space. Why could not I in thought annihilate space ? This was the puzzle; and it remained a puzzle to me till, in after years, I began to study Kant. Kant gave an explanation; but the explanation he gave commits us to such sweeping idealistic consequences that, even to this day, I cannot accept it.

After leaving the spiritual atmosphere of Collace, and going to reside at Banchory, where I had to associate constantly with people in a great measure indifferent to divine things, my spirituality ere long began gradually to decline. Along with this, as a natural consequence, my former peace and happiness declined, and I often exclaimed, in the language of the poet Cowper—

" What peaceful hours I once enjoyed !
How sweet their memory still;
But they have left an aching void
The world can never fill."

On leaving Banchory, and returning home, I was again in a more congenial atmosphere.

At this time the controversy between Arminianism and Calvinism was beginning to agitate the country. I took a very keen interest in the controversy, adopting the Arminian side of the question. When I went to the west of Scotland, I naturally associated myself with the Arminians, then called Morisonians, for at this time the Evangelical Union had not been formed.

When I went to Paisley, they were endeavouring to establish a congregation in the town. I took a lively interest in the work. Mr. Landels, now the well-known Rev. Dr. Landels of Edinburgh, then a student of Mr. Morison, Kilmarnock, preached frequently and with much success; he was a most excellent young man, but he soon adopted Baptist principles. After him Mr. A. M. Wilson, now the esteemed pastor of the E.U. Church, Bathgate, came and preached for some time with success; and when the church was formed, he was chosen as the pastor. From a manuscript list of the members, I find that I had been elected as one of the deacons; but I never acted in this capacity, as I left the place just after the church had been organised.

I may here mention, that on coming to Paisley I felt somewhat disappointed at a very marked difference between the Arminians of the West and the Calvinists of Collace, with whom I had formerly associated. The former were more argumentative; but they were not so spiritual, so fond of the social prayer-meeting, or so much inclined to speak to one another of their own personal experiences. This may be accounted for by the fact that at Collace there had been a genuine revival of religion, while in the west there had been simply a revival of Arminian principles. This difference did not, however, lessen my conviction of the truth of the Arminian principles.

To resume my narrative: After coming home from Paisley, I had to consider what was to be done to enable me to earn a livelihood for the future. I had not received the proper training, or the sort of education which would fit me for becoming a clerk; and, even supposing I had, it was a kind of occupation for which I was naturally unsuited. After some consideration, it was thought that some sort of occupation in the tea trade might suit me. On duly thinking over the matter, I went to Perth to see what could be done. I had come to no conclusion as to whom I should consult, or as to what shop I should enter. Musing over the matter, as I approached the city by the bridge, I observed a man distributing small handbills to the passers-by. All in a moment it struck me that if these bills should relate to the tea trade, I would be guided by this, and would go to the shop to which they referred; at least, before trying any other. What could induce me to come to a conclusion so apparently absurd and incautious, I cannot tell. Strange are the ways of Providence! for had it not been for that decision, in all probability, my future course in life would have been very different from what it actually turned out to be. On coming up to the man, I found the bills related to a tea and coffee warehouse which had recently been opened in the High Street of Perth. Guided by the bill, I went direct to the shop, and found the proprietor to be an agreeable and intelligent person. After talking over various matters, I then told him what I had been thinking about. He agreed with me that I might manage to make a comfortable livelihood by selling tea; and that I might push the sale by going into the country. I accordingly got a small stock and commenced operations. I soon found, however, that the attempt to push a sale in the country was a rather disagreeable job for me, and I resolved to give it up. The merchant whom I had visited—Mr. David Irons, who afterwards proved to be one of the kindest friends I have ever met with in life—now proposed to me that I might try and open a shop for myself in some suitable town, where I might be likely to succeed. Unfortunately, I had not the means for any such undertaking; but he, in the most kindly manner, offered to assist me. He agreed to give me a stock to commence with, and that I should repay him in regular instalments as it was sold; and that he would in this way keep up my stock. I need hardly say that an offer so generous was readily accepted. As it was now about the end of the harvest season, my friend suggested that I might come to Perth for the winter, and learn the mechanical art of weighing and parcelling up the tea, serving over the counter, and all the usual routine of shop work. I accordingly came in; and, before the winter was over, I became a thoroughly proficient shopkeeper.

On the approach of spring 1847, it was arranged that I should try Elgin, as a likely place. I accordingly went north, secured a suitable shop, and commenced business. As the merchants there were charging large profits, I soon secured a fair amount of trade. I liked the place, my occupation, and the people very much. The shop work suited me well, as it afforded intervals now and again for reading and study. I had not long entered on my new occupation when an incident occurred which I may now mention, as it led to consequences which very much influenced my opinions on theological subjects. Although I had read a good deal on the free will controversy, I had never seen Edwards' famous work on the subject. One day, however, I went out to a bookseller, purchased this treatise, came back to the shop, and commenced reading it. I had not proceeded far before I became much impressed by the singular acuteness, clearness, and force of the reasoning. It excited feelings approaching to astonishment and admiration. I resolved then to commence at the beginning of the book and study it through, line by line, and page by page, until I should thoroughly master the treatise. This I did with the greatest care, often lingering for a day on a single page, with the view of not only thoroughly mastering the argument, but of examining it under every possible phase. But after I had gone through the book in this manner, I was utterly unable to perceive a flaw in the reasoning, which could in any way vitiate the main conclusions. The whole appeared irresistibly clear and convincing; and yet I could not adopt the theory that man was a necessitated agent. I went over the book a second, a third, a fourth, a fifth, and more times, with the self-same result. In short, for at least a year and a half, every spare hour of the day was devoted to the study of this work. It is probable that no one has ever devoted so much time to the study of the book as I have done. It is the most fascinating book I have ever met with in all my studies.

I had heard a good deal about Professor Tappan, of America, who had published a refutation of Edwards' arguments. I accordingly ordered a copy; and after a delay of several weeks, Tappan's work, consisting of three volumes, came to hand. I eagerly set to work to study Tappan's examination of Edwards' system, with the hope and expectation that I would now be enabled to perceive Edwards' fundamental error; for I still believed that an error somewhere must exist. But I had not gone far into the book, when I began to perceive, to my disappointment, not only that my difficulties were not met, but that Tappan had failed to perceive the real nature of the problem, or the force of Edwards' main argument against a self-determining power in the will. When I had read the second volume on the appeal to consciousness, my disappointment was not diminished. The testimony of consciousness, according to Tappan, seemed to amount simply to this: " I am perfectly conscious when I choose A., for example, of having the conviction that, all things else being the same, I might have chosen B. instead of A." This no one will deny; but it leaves wholly undetermined the question as to whether the conviction is true or false; and this is the very point in dispute. The impression produced in my mind by the reading of Tappan's work was that the assumed flaw in the reasoning of Edwards had really no existence. Since then I have gone over thirty or forty treatises on the free will controversy, the most of which were opposed to Edwards, and my conviction as to the soundness of Edwards' conclusions remains unchanged. As a natural consequence, all my former objections to the main points of the Calvinistic theology soon disappeared; and I became convinced that some moderate form of Calvinism was nearest the truth, not only of philosophy, but also of Scripture.

I must here refer to a thought which suggested itself to my mind shortly after commencing the study of Edwards' treatise. The idea was this: the determination in reference to the will is merely a special form of a far more general and comprehensive system of determination, in fact, a determination which comprehends universal nature. Every organic form in nature is what it is, in virtue of determination. Whether it is a plant or an animal, or whatever else its specific size, form, genus, and every peculiarity may be—everything is due to the particular determination given to the molecules in its formation. The fundamental question in reference to the production of organic forms is not—What are the forces in action, or on what does their exertion depend? but, What is that which directs or determines these forces, what directs their action? It is not—What moves the molecules in the production of the organic form? but, What determines that motion? It is the particular determination of the force which accounts for the particular phenomenon. The mere exertion of force may be supposed to be the same in all phenomena. And what holds true of the physical world holds equally true of the mental, moral, and spiritual. In short, the entire universe is a process of determinations, but not of determinations occurring at random. There are a unity, a plan, and a purpose pervading the whole, which imply thought and intelligence. When these considerations suggested themselves to my mind, I was very much impressed; and I resolved that I would go into the examination of this subject, and devote my future time, in so far as it was at my command, to this work. Unfortunately, however, I did not abide by my resolution; for I allowed physical science to divert my mind from the matter for fully a quarter of a century of the best part of my life.

On the 11th September 1848, I was married to my wife, Isabella, second youngest daughter of Mr. John Macdonald, Forres. The union has proved a happy one. She has been the sharer of my joys, sorrows, and trials (and these have not been few) for the past forty years. Her care, economy, and kindly attention to my comfort during the years of comparative hardships through which we have passed, have cheered me on during all my trials and sorrows.

At this time I was addicted to the nasty habit of smoking tobacco. I had only smoked for a few years, but the appetite seems to have got a strong hold of me. The tobacco had a most injurious effect on my stomach and nervous system. I had lost almost all appetite for food, and was altogether in a somewhat shaky condition. I had repeatedly tried to abandon the habit, but without success. At last I determined that, come what might, I would never during my life put a pipe in my mouth, and that, to make this determination more binding on me, I would pledge myself in writing to do so. I mentioned this resolution to one or two friends, who were about as great slaves to the tobacco as myself; and they agreed to follow my example. Accordingly, a pledge was written out, to which we appended our names. From that day, 29th December 1849, till the present hour, I have adhered strictly to my pledge. I believe, however, that I am the only one of those who signed the pledge who so adhered to it. I had a terrible struggle with the appetite. For two or three months I was in a state of partial stupor, and it was nearly three years before the craving for the tobacco left me.

I may mention that I had been a pledged abstainer from drink for several years before then. In fact, as drink was not used at home by my parents, I may say that I was practically an abstainer from infancy.

A little after the time at which I gave up the use of tobacco, my elbow joint, which had not troubled me since the time I left Paisley, was attacked by inflammation of a very serious character. The effect of the inflammation was to completely destroy the joint, which shortly afterwards ossified, and became immovable. This was a sad blow to me; but, like many more of the strange dispensations of Providence, it proved a blessing in disguise. It completely cured the joint disease, and I afterwards enjoyed better health. By this illness, however, I was so long unfitted for attendance in my shop, that the trade rapidly fell off; and afterwards I could not manage to get the business raised to a paying condition. I struggled on for some time; but at last, in order to avoid losing money and getting into debt, I resolved to close the shop. I accordingly sold off everything, left Elgin, and came south to Perth. This was about the beginning of the summer of 1850. Owing to the weakly state of my arm, it was a considerable time after coming south before I was able to do any manual work. At that time the influence of electricity and galvanism as a curative agent was exciting a good deal of attention. As I was familiar with the construction of the machines which were used, I thought I should try the making of an induction apparatus, which I accordingly did. It was soon purchased; and, as others were required, I continued at the making of them for some time.

For about a year, at this period, I had a great deal

of leisure time for reading and study. My principal reading was on questions relating to liberty and necessity. This led me into theology, and then into metaphysics. I began at this time to study the Scottish school, and read, as I could get access to books, Reid, Stewart, Brown, Hamilton, and others. One of the first books I read was Beattie on Truth, which much delighted me, as it tended to remove a sort of philosophical scepticism and doubt in regard to the foundations of certainty, which made me often feel rather unhappy.

Again, however, the great question to be considered was to what hand I should turn in order to earn a permanent livelihood. Some of my friends suggested that I should try a temperance hotel; and one of them stated that he was about to erect a house at Blairgowrie, and that I could have it for that purpose if I chose. After due consideration I made up my mind to try that course. But here was the difficulty: the house required to be furnished, and this would require a considerable sum, which I had not. It occurred to me, however, that, as it would be some six or eight months before the house could be ready for occupation, and as my arm was now much improved, I might try and make a considerable number of the necessary articles of furniture during that time. I accordingly set to work: made chairs, tables, bedsteads, basin-stands, toilet-tables, and other articles; and, with the small sum in our possession, we managed to open the house in the early part of 1852. As we had no family, my wife, anxious to lessen expenses as much as possible, proposed to dispense with a servant, and do all the work herself. The house was kept in the perfection of cleanliness, and every attention was paid to the comfort of visitors, who generally expressed themselves well pleased. But as there was no railway to Blairgowrie at that time, the visitors were few and far between; and it was only with the most strict economy that we could manage to keep out of debt. Although Mrs. Croll had too much work, I, on the contrary, unfortunately had too little. I took it into my foolish head to try to learn the Latin language. The reader will smile when I tell him that my main aim in trying to acquire Latin was to enable me to read the discussions of the schoolmen. An assistant teacher in the parish school gave me three lessons a week privately. But it would be difficult to find one with less aptitude for languages than I have. With a great amount of labour and perseverance I managed, in the course of a year, to acquire a knowledge of the rudiments of the language, and was reading in Cæsar. I found, however, that I would require another year's study before my Latin would be sufficient for my purpose; and, as I could not afford to lose so much time, I abandoned the whole affair.

After a year and a half's trial of the hotel, we found that there was little chance of its ever becoming self-supporting; so we gave it up, sold the furniture, and left the place. This was at the May term of 1853. I then went to Glasgow, where I obtained employment in an insurance office. About this time the Safety Life Assurance Company was started. This company was under the directorship of Richard Cobden, John Bright, Henry E. Gurney, Thomas Brassey, and other well-known men. A friend of mine, Mr. Wm. Logan, much esteemed in Glasgow for the interest he took in the temperance and other social reforms, was appointed the agent for the company in Glasgow. Requiring an assistant, he offered me the place, which I accepted. My principal duties were outside the office, pushing for proposals, in which I was pretty successful, particularly among the working classes. During the summer of the following year, cholera broke out very badly in Glasgow; and as the company was desirous that business should be as much suspended as possible till the epidemic should somewhat abate, I left the town for a few weeks and went to Perth. While at Perth, Dr. Robert D. Thomson, the well-known chemist, who was one of the directors of the Temperance Provident Institution, was there on a visit at the time. The directors of this institution wished an agent in Dundee to devote his whole time to the work, and as something about my qualifications was known, I was offered the appointment. The terms proposed to me were favourable. I accepted the offer, went down to Dundee about the end of August, and commenced operations. I succeeded pretty well in that town. After I had been about nine or ten months in the place, the directors of the Safety Office offered me their Edinburgh agency; and as the situation was much superior, so far as salary was concerned, to that which I then held, I of course accepted the appointment, and at the May term of 1855, left Dundee for Edinburgh.

I found it much more difficult to obtain assurance proposals in Edinburgh than in either Glasgow or Dundee. The Safety was an English company, new and untried; and although the directors were well-known men, it did not offer any advantages superior or even equal to those of some of the old-established Edinburgh offices.

In the spring of 1856 my father died. There is something impressive about the death of one's parents. It brings forcibly to mind the fact that we are here but pilgrims and strangers.

During the time I was in the insurance business, I managed to find a considerable amount of time for reading and study. This was effected by employing every moment of my extra office hours to this purpose. My reading was exclusively in philosophy. It was in Edinburgh that I began the study of Kant. With the exception of Edwards, no writer has made such an impression on my mind as Kant.

At this time I became very much troubled by pain in the eyes, occasioned by looking so much on white paper. When the pain began in the eyes, strange to say, it left the top or opening of the head, the place where it had been seated almost from infancy. I found that, by placing a small piece of plain coloured glass on the page of the book, I could manage to read without feeling much inconvenience. The pain in the eyes continued for several years.

In the autumn of 1856 I was transferred from Edinburgh to Leicester, where it was expected that more business might be done. When I came to Leicester, I found that there was as much difficulty in obtaining proposals there as in Edinburgh. Although one of the members of Parliament for the town was a director of the company, yet the people of Leicester seemed to think that one of the old-established Scotch offices was fully as safe as the Safety. After being there for about six months, my wife took seriously ill, and the medical advisers stated that it would be necessary that she should leave Leicester when she was able to be removed. She was shortly afterwards removed to Glasgow, to be beside her sisters, and there she lay for upwards of a year in bed.

As I could not return to Leicester, and the company had no opening for me in Scotland, I left their service. I got an engagement again from the Temperance Provident Institution, and went to Paisley, where I remained for six or eight months. I then finally abandoned the insurance business altogether, after spending four and a half years of about the most disagreeable part of my life. To one like me, naturally so fond of retirement and even of solitude, it was painful to be constantly obliged to make up to strangers.

I was now at perfect leisure, and as, for some time, nothing turned up for me to do, I commenced and drew up, somewhat hastily, some thoughts on the metaphysics of theism, a subject over which I had been pondering. These were embodied in the small volume, published anonymously in the latter end of 1857, under the title, *The Philosophy of Theism.* Only five hundred copies were printed, and the most of them were circulated privately. The book, though favourably received by the press, attracted but little general attention. It appeared at a time when metaphysics was at about its lowest ebb.

In the spring of the following year, 1858, I got an engagement in the office of the *Commonwealth*, a Glasgow weekly newspaper, principally devoted to the advocacy of temperance, and social and political reform. On the 29th August of the same year my mother died; and my brother David, who up till this time had been residing at home with her at Wolfhill, came through and took up his abode with us. As I mentioned before, he was deformed, being hunchbacked, in consequence, as it was supposed, of a fall received when an infant.

A few months after my mother's death I unfortunately met with a mishap which has since entailed on me a considerable amount of pain and discomfort, and has disabled me all along for much physical exertion. One day, as I was exerting my whole strength in using a joiner's plane, while dressing a piece of wood, something suddenly appeared to give way about the region of the heart. Medical men have never been able to detect what is wrong. But ever since then, though my health and strength remained unimpaired, I durst not lift anything heavy, or attempt to run, or even walk fast. This mishap, however, has been to me a far less affliction than one which happened seven years later, and to which I shall afterwards have occasion to refer.

After remaining for upwards of a year and a half in the *Commonwealth* office, I learned that a person was required to take charge of Anderson's College and Museum, and applied for the situation. There were about sixty applicants. Fortunately for me, as it afterwards turned out, I received the appointment, and entered on my duties at the end of the autumn of 1859. Taking it all in all, I have never been in any place so congenial to me as that institution proved. After upwards of twenty years of an unsettled life, full of hardships and difficulties, it was a relief to get settled down in what might be regarded as a permanent home. My salary was small, it is true, little more than sufficient to enable us to subsist; but this was compensated by advantages for me of another kind. It will naturally be asked—why such want of success in life? Why so many changes, trials, and difficulties? There were several causes which conspired to lead to this state of things. The mishap to my elbow joint compelled me to give up the occupation of a joiner when a young man; and the inflammation which destroyed the joint five years afterwards had the effect of blasting my hopes in the way of shopkeeping. The main cause, however, and one of which I had been all along conscious, was that strong and almost irresistible propensity towards study, which prevented me devoting my whole energy to business. Study always came first, business second; and the result was that in this age of competition I was left behind in the race. In this respect, however, my situation in Anderson's College suited me well. Here was the fine scientific library, belonging to the Glasgow Philosophical Society, to which I had access,—a privilege of which I took due advantage. Here also was the library of four or five thousand volumes in connection with the popular evening classes of the institution; and, further, the private library of the founder of the institution, consisting of over two thousand volumes. My duties were regular and steady, requiring little mental labour; and as my brother was staying with me, he gave me a great deal of assistance, which consequently allowed me a good deal of spare time for study. The Museum was open from 11 A.M. till 3 P.M.; but as I had little or nothing to do with the arrangement and classification of the specimens, and there were but few visitors, I had generally a few hours a day of a quiet time for reading and study.

I suspect that the fact of my mind being so evenly balanced between the love of physics and the love of philosophy has been a disadvantage as well as an advantage to me; for when I am engaged in physics, for example, I am continually tempted to turn aside into philosophy; and when in philosophy, the attractions of physics frequently draw me over. In fact, it is only by a strong effort of will that I have managed to keep for years continuously in the same region of inquiry, without passing over into the other.

When I came to Anderson's College, I had been engaged in philosophical and theological studies for a period of fifteen years. Just about the time I entered the institution, I had, in fact, begun to consider in a systematic form the problem which, as already stated, had suggested itself to my mind in 1848, and which had been but slightly touched upon in my little book, *The Philosophy of Theism*, then recently published. I soon found, however, that the attractions offered by the institution for the study of physical science were too strong to allow me to continue my metaphysical studies; and although this problem to which I had set myself was then, as it still is, the one of all others most attractive to me, I nevertheless resolved to lay it aside for a year or two, and begin again the study of physics at the place where I had left it off in former years. At this time, the then modern principle of the transformation and conservation of energy and the dynamical theory of heat attracted my attention. I read also with much interest the researches of Faraday, Joule, Thomson, Tyndall, Rankine, and others on heat, electricity, and magnetism. At this period the question of the cause of the Glacial epoch was being discussed with interest among geologists. In the spring of 1864 I turned my attention to this subject; and, without knowing at the time what Herschel and Lyell had written on the matter, it occurred to me that the change in the eccentricity of the earth's orbit might probably be the real cause. I accordingly drew up a paper on the subject, which was published in the *Philosophical Magazine* for August 1864. The paper excited a considerable amount of attention, and I was repeatedly advised to go more fully into the subject; and, as the path appeared to me a new and interesting one, I resolved to follow it out. But little did I suspect, at the time when I made this resolution, that it would become a path so entangled that fully twenty years would elapse before I could get out of it.

One evening in July of 1865, after a day's writing, I hurriedly bent down to assist in putting a few tacks into a carpet, when I experienced something like a twitch in a part of the upper and left side of the head. It did not strike me at the time as a matter of much importance; but it afterwards proved to be the severest affliction that has happened to me in life. Had it not been for this mishap to the head, all the private work I have been able to do during the twenty years which followed might have easily been done, and would have been done, in the course of two or three years. The affection in the head did not in any way affect my general health, neither did it in the least degree impair my mental energy. I could think as vigorously as ever, but I dared not " turn on the full steam." After this twitch a dull pain settled in that part of the brain, which increased till it became unbearable, if I persisted in doing mental work for any length of time. I was therefore obliged to do mental labour very quietly and slowly, for a short period at a time, and then take a good long rest. If I attempted to do too much in one day, I was generally disabled for a few days to come. Another consequence was this: before this affliction in my head, I could concentrate my thoughts on a single point, and exert my whole mental energy till the difficulty was overcome; but this I never could attempt afterwards. After struggling so many years against difficulties of every sort, and just at the time I had about overcome them all, and was expecting to be able to do some real work, I felt it very hard to be so disabled for the future. However, under all these difficulties, I managed, during the two and a half years which elapsed before I left Anderson's College, to write about a dozen of papers of a longer or shorter character.

Amongst the very first to express a favourable opinion of the theory of the cause of the Glacial epoch, which I had recently advanced in the *Philosophical Magazine*, were Professor (now Sir Andrew) Ramsay, then director of the Geological Survey of England and Wales, and Dr. A. Geikie, who, on the reorganisation of the service, had just been appointed to the directorship of the Scottish Survey. At this time a large addition to the staff was required, and I was asked if I would be willing to allow myself to be nominated for the Scottish service. This very kind offer was tempting to me in many respects; but as I was somewhat up in years, and suffering a little from the mishap to my head, and, besides, not satisfied as to my special qualifications for the scientific duties of the office, I did not see my way clear to accept the proposal. As it was necessary that one of the men should be permanently located in Edinburgh, to act as resident surveyor and clerk in the office, I was again asked if I would be willing to accept this appointment. This very materially altered the condition of things; and, after duly thinking over the matter, and consulting some of my friends, I agreed to be nominated. I felt, how- ever, reluctant to undertake duties which required much mental work, as, owing to the state of my head, it might materially interfere with the private work on which my mind was so much set. But, on the other hand, as my salary was so small, and my health at the same time suffering a good deal during the winter months from the cold draughts in the lobbies of the institution, I felt that, taking all things into consideration, I ought not to lose this opportunity of improving my circumstances, and I accordingly agreed to stand for Civil Service examination. I failed, however, in some of the subjects. This is what might have been expected, considering my constitutional nervousness, combined with my age and want of experience in ordeals of that kind. I, notwithstanding, received the appointment, and got my Civil Service certificate some time afterwards. I accordingly resigned my situation in Glasgow, went through to Edinburgh, and entered the Service on September 2, 1867.

I found, as I had expected, that the duties of the office were not at all laborious, either physically or mentally. They consisted simply in attending to the various details of office work: namely, conducting the correspondence with the men in the field; supplying them with the necessary maps, instruments, and stores; correspondence with the engraver, colourist, and Ordnance Survey; checking the maps; keeping the registers, etc. etc. These various duties kept me busy during office hours, without producing mental exhaustion. The only thing I suffered from was now and again having to write two or three letters in succession. The director, Mr. Geikie, I found to be a most agreeable person. This was all along a great comfort to me. During the thirteen years we were together in the office, never so much as an angry word passed between us. I need hardly add that my duties as resident geologist really did not require much acquaintance with the science of geology. This relieved my mind from having to study a science for which I had no great liking, and thus allowed me to devote my whole leisure hours to those physical questions in which I was engaged. There was, however, one department of geological inquiry with which the physical questions, in which I was then engaged, required that I should be acquainted, namely, surface geology, or drift in its bearings on Glacial and Interglacial periods. I had begun my studies in this department before I left the " Andersonian," and had made frequent excursions into the country in search of glacial phenomena. I was fortunate in discovering two remarkable buried river channels, belonging to pre-Glacial and Interglacial ages, and some other singular facts bearing on the history of the Glacial period. These researches were continued after I went to Edinburgh with equal success; and their results were given in one or two papers contributed to magazines, and afterwards embodied in *Climate and Time.*

Although the hours of business in my new occupation were not long—being only from 10 A.M. to 4 P.M.—and the duties not laborious, I nevertheless found that in the evening I was not in such a fresh condition to begin my private labours as I was when in the " Andersonian."

This at times made me feel a sort of half regret that I had ever left my former situation. These six hours of mental work, comparatively light as it certainly was, added to my private work, began ere long to tell badly on my poor head; and I had to adopt every means I could devise to husband my energies.

I may here give a short statement of the mode of life which I adopted when I came to Edinburgh, to which I adhered pretty closely during the whole time I was in the Survey. After being in Edinburgh for a short time, I took a small house at Jordan Bank, Morningside, at the southern extremity of the city. After coming home from the office and taking dinner, which was generally about five o'clock in the afternoon, I took a rest for about an hour, and then took a stroll in the country. A few hundred yards beyond Morningside the main road separates into two branches, which, after diverging about a quarter of a mile apart, again unite about a mile and a half beyond the place where they separated. One very frequent walk of mine after dinner was to go out by the one branch and return by the other. This gave me a circuit of about three miles. As I walked very slowly and employed the whole time in study, I was generally out of doors for one hour and a half, or two hours. At other times I would make an excursion to the Braid Hills or to Craiglockhart. As the beauties of nature, especially in its retirement, have such a charm for me, I found these outdoor walks helpful to study. I never took a companion with me in these walks, as not only would doing so deprive me of the opportunity of getting on with my studies, but the effort and excitement of talking would to a considerable extent unfit my head for mental work on my return.

In these walks I generally carried a pencil in the one hand and a bit of paper in the other, on which I jotted down my ideas as they suggested themselves; or rather, I should say, made jottings to enable me to keep a record of them till my return home, when they would be written out more fully. To save my head, I got a young man to come and read and write an hour each evening for me. This generally would end the labours of the day. But, should I be still in a working condition, I would continue my studies quietly for another hour.

I found that if I attempted to do any head work in the morning, it would completely knock me up for the day. When going to the office in the morning, I was obliged, as much as possible, to avoid talking to people on the way, which sometimes was no easy matter; and this compelled me to take a by-path. Another thing I was obliged to adopt, was not going out to public meetings or to dinner or evening parties. Had I not adopted this mode of life, I could not, in the state of my head, have done private work. During the thirteen years I was in Edinburgh, I remember of being only twice at a scientific meeting, and once at a concert. On the whole, I led a somewhat retired life in Edinburgh. But, in order to get on with my work, I had to adopt another expedient: namely, to confine my reading exclusively to the subjects which I was engaged in studying. So strictly did I adhere to this resolution, that it was but rarely I looked even at a newspaper or a journal of any kind. In fact, my reading was rather a toil to me than a pleasure. It was a means to an end, but a means which could not be avoided. The pleasure lay in the study, and not in the reading; but without the reading there would not have been sufficient materials for study. Had

I been reading simply for pleasure, it would probably not have been either in physics or in metaphysics, but rather in the writings of Wordsworth, Tennyson, and other authors of that *ideal* type.

In all my reading I had to adopt this plan: namely, to mark on the margin of the page, and underline with pencil the passages to which I might have occasion to refer. Had I not adopted this mode, the reading would not have been of great advantage. But, notwithstanding all these precautions, the head grew gradually worse; so much so, that I had frequently to apply for sick leave for a month or six weeks at a time; and in 1873 I was disabled for duty for nearly nine months. For two or three years prior to the publication of *Climate and Time*, it was with the greatest difficulty that I could manage to put together in one day as many sentences as would fill half a page of foolscap. In fact, the appearance of the volume was delayed for two or three years on this account. During all this time the mind was as vigorous as ever; it was pain in the head, and pain alone, which stopped all progress when I attempted mental work. I frequently thought I should be obliged to resign my situation in the Survey; but as I had not completed my tenth year of service, and would therefore not be entitled to superannuation, I was strongly urged to try and struggle on. I was for several years under the medical treatment of Dr. Warburton Begbie, and this experienced physician did everything in his power; but nothing he could prescribe had any effect. I was afterwards under Professor Sanders, and latterly under Professor Grainger Stewart, with no greater success.

In February 1876, my brother, who had been staying with us ever since my mother's death, died suddenly from heart disease. In this same month the University of St. Andrews conferred on me the degree of LL.D., an honour which I felt at the time somewhat doubtful as to the propriety of accepting. A few months afterwards I was elected a Fellow of the Royal Society of London.

I may also mention that in the same year I was chosen an Honorary Member of the New York Academy of Science. I was afterwards chosen an Honorary Member of the Bristol Natural Society, of the Psychological Society of Great Britain, of the Glasgow Geological Society, of the Literary and Antiquarian Society of Perth, and of the Perthshire Society of Natural Science. I had the honour of receiving from the Geological Society of London the balance of the proceeds of the Wollaston Donation Fund in 1872, the Murchison Fund in 1876, and the Barlow-Jamieson Fund in 1884.

When I had finished *Climate and Time*, I resolved to abandon not only my climatological studies, but physics in general, in order to be able to resume those investigations into the philosophy of evolution, which I had laid aside at the time that I entered Anderson's College. I soon found, however, that it was a resolution to which I could not well adhere. After the publication of the volume, I found that, notwithstanding the care I had taken to express my views in the clearest manner I could, these views were on many points very much mis-apprehended. I therefore found it necessary to endeavour not only to remove those misapprehensions, but to enter at much greater length into some of those difficult points which had perhaps been too briefly discussed in the volume. The consequence was, that, owing to the state of my head obliging me to write so slowly, and also to other circumstances, it was not till 1885, or ten years after the publication of the volume, that I managed to shake myself clear of that perplexing question which had engaged my attention for upwards of twenty years. (Since this was written, I have been obliged to enter again into the consideration of some points.—May 1888.)

One day in the office, during the summer of 1880, while hurriedly endeavouring to remove some maps from a drawer, and standing in an awkward position on a pair of steps, I unfortunately strained something about the region of the heart. The result was, that for months

I was unable to walk about, or make any physical exertion. It became doubtful if I should ever be able for office duties. Just at this time, I had been suffering rather badly from my old complaint in the head, and was at the time under the medical treatment of Professor Grainger Stewart. This gentleman thought that it might be well to try what effect the external application of that powerful drug aconite might have in relieving the pain in the affected part of the head. His instructions were to apply a little of the aconite over the part when I felt the pain badly. I continued to do so for some time, but it had not the desired effect. One evening, after I had applied it once or twice, I all at once found that I had lost my power of speech, or rather, that I could only speak like a paralytic, in an unintelligible form. It is evident that this powerful poison had paralysed some of the nerves or muscles of the tongue or the lips. In course of a week or two I regained my speech, though even yet there are a good many words which I cannot pronounce.

As I was now disabled for duty both by head and heart, and as there was not much prospect that I should ever be fit for office work, it was considered advisable that I should resign. And as I had been admitted into the service at the advanced age of forty-six, it was believed that, in computing the amount of superannuation to be allotted me, my age would be taken into consideration. This I had every reason to believe would be the case, the more so, seeing that there was a clause in the Superannuation Act which applied to my case. I accordingly agreed to withdraw from service. But, to my utter chagrin, no attention was paid to these considerations by the Treasury; and I received superannuation only for the thirteen years I had actually been in the Service. Thus my income was all at once reduced from £350 to £75, 16s. 8d. a year. No effort was made to urge upon the Treasury to allow me a little more; and as this sum was insufficient, seeing that I was a married man, I had no alternative but to give up housekeeping and go into cheap lodgings. Application was made to Mr. Gladstone, who was then Prime Minister and First Lord of the Treasury, to allow me a small sum from the Civil List; but, after keeping my friends waiting for a year and a half, he stated that he could not recommend a pension for me. A year or two afterwards, when Lord Salisbury came into office, application was again made by my friends for a small grant from the Civil List, but with like unsuccess.

After moving about for five years in this unsettled condition, and having during the time obtained, through the kindness of friends, a little increase to my income, I resolved on taking up house again. I was fortunate in obtaining a lease of a comfortable house in the suburbs of Perth; and, at the end of the summer of 1886, I took up my permanent abode there.

The results of my labours since the appearance of *Climate and Time* in 1875 were, in October of 1885, published in a volume, under the title of *Climate and Cosmology*. This I resolved should terminate my studies, not merely in climatology, but also in physical science in general. This resolution, as was stated before, was made in order to enable me to finish work which had been laid aside for upwards of twenty-five years. But whether my wish in this respect will ever be accomplished, is certainly at present a matter of uncertainty.

CHAPTER I

ANCESTRY, BIRTH, CHILDHOOD, AND SCHOOL DAYS

"AMONG all the provinces in Scotland," writes Sir Walter Scott, "if an intelligent stranger were asked to describe the most varied and the most beautiful, it is probable he would name the county of Perth. A native, also, of any other district of Caledonia, though his partialities might lead him to prefer his native county in the first instance, would certainly class that of Perth in the second, and thus give its inhabitants a fair right to plead that—prejudice apart—Perthshire forms the fairest portion of the northern kingdom. It is long since Lady Mary Wortley Montagu, with that excellent taste which characterises her writings, expressed her opinion that the most interesting district of every country, and that which exhibits the varied beauties of natural scenery in greatest perfection, is that where the mountains sink down upon the champaign, or more level land. The most picturesque, if not the highest hills, are to be found in the county of Perth. The rivers find their way out of the mountainous region by the wildest leaps, and through the most romantic passes connecting the Highlands with the Lowlands. Above, the vegetation of a happier climate and soil is mingled with the magnificent characteristics of mountain scenery ; and woods, groves, and thickets in profusion clothe the base of the hills, ascend up the ravines, and mingle with the precipices. It is in such favoured regions that the traveller finds what the poet Gray, or someone else, has termed ' beauty lying in the lap of terror.'

" From the same advantage of situation, this favoured province presents a variety of the most pleasing character. Its lakes, woods, and mountains vie in beauty with any that the Highland tour exhibits; while Perthshire contains amidst this romantic scenery, and in some places in connection with it, many fertile and habitable tracts which may vie with the richness of Merry England herself. The country has also been the scene of many remarkable exploits and events, some of historical importance, others interesting to the poet and romancer, though recorded in popular tradition alone. It was in these vales that the Saxons of the plain and the Gael of the mountains had many a desperate and bloody encounter, in which it was frequently impossible to decide the palm of victory between the mailed chivalry of the low country and the plaided clans whom they opposed."[1]

In the eastern division of this charming county lies the little post-office village of Cargill, which gives its name to a parish in one of the most picturesque districts, known as Strathmore. The village stands on the left bank of the river Tay, about three quarters of a mile west-south-west of the railway station of Cargill on the Caledonian line, being about eleven and a half miles north-north-east of the city of Perth, and four and a quarter miles south-west of the town of Coupar-Angus.

The parish embraces the villages of Burreltown, Woodside, and Wolfhill, and is bounded on the north-east by Coupar-Angus, on the east by Kettins, in Forfarshire, and by a detached portion of Scone, on the south-east by Abernyte and Collace, on the south by St. Martins, on the west by Auchtergaven and Kinclaven, and on the north-west by Caputh. Its greatest length, from east-north-east to west-south-west, is about $6\frac{3}{8}$ miles; its breadth, from north-west to south-east, varies between $3\frac{1}{2}$ furlongs and 5 miles; and its area is $9626\frac{1}{2}$ acres, of which $131\frac{1}{2}$ are water. The noble river Tay,

[1] *Fair Maid of Perth.*

which pours the largest volume of water into the ocean of any river in Great Britain, and was compared by the early Roman invaders with the Tiber, winds its way for four and a half miles along the western boundary of the parish, while the lazy little Isla, gliding for two and a quarter miles down to the Tay, traces the north-western boundary. The land is finely diversified with ascents and declivities, clad with wood and interspersed with water. The western border, to the mean breadth of about a mile, rises gradually from the Tay,—the central tracts forming a low plateau with some unevenness of contour, while the eastern border includes a strip of the Sidlaw Hills. In the extreme south-west the surface sinks to about 100 feet above sea-level, thence rising near Wolfhill to a height of 409 feet, of 414 feet in Gallowhill, of 390 feet at Redstone, of 598 feet near Legertlaw, and of about 1235 in King's Seat on the Abernyte border. Sandstone of excellent quality has been extensively quarried for building purposes, and limestone is to be found in considerable quantity, which might be profitably worked, whilst a reddish rock marl is also plentiful in the district. The soil near the Tay is strongly argillaceous; on the central plateau it is partly loamy and partly moorish; while towards the foot of the Sidlaws it is formed of light, dry gravel. An extensive acreage is under wood, very little is pastoral, and still less is allowed to lie waste. The scenery along the Tay includes the picturesque Linn of Campsie, and ranges from the softly romantic to the grandly magnificent. Tumuli and remains of Caledonian megalithic structures occur in various places, while vestiges of a Roman camp, with *fossæ* perfectly discernible, and with fragments of an aqueduct leading from it to a neighbouring rivulet, are to be seen near the confluence of the Tay and Isla. A Roman road, twenty feet broad, and formed of rough, round stones, passes north-eastward by Burreltown; and a high rock overlooking the Linn of Campsie is crowned by traces of an ancient monastery, said to have been subordinate to Cupar, whose abbey, being supplied with fuel from Campsie Wood, gives the name of Abbey Road to the track by which it was conveyed. Stobhall House, a prominent feature, belongs to Lady Willoughby de Eresby, who is the largest proprietor in the district.

At Little Whitefield, a small hamlet in this charming county, James Croll was born on Tuesday the 2nd of January 1821, at eleven o'clock at night. The weather was cold and stormy, with snow lying thickly on the ground, as in the case of Burns, who sings—

> " 'Twas then a blast of Januar' win'
> Blew hansel in on Robin."

The war of the elements seems to have foretold the troubled and unsettled life which Croll was destined to lead, as well as the comparatively cold reception which his last work was doomed to meet from the unsympathetic world. . . . Most instructive would it be, were we able to tell the history of his ancestors on both sides of the family, as has been so fully done in the case of Ralph Waldo Emerson, and see how nature, working quietly through many years and gathering from many sources, at last produced, by the blending of many different qualifications, the man in whom the family was destined to develop its noblest mental and moral characteristics, and then to pass away. Unfortunately, of his ancestors on the mother's side, we know almost nothing. On the father's side Croll seems to have been the consummate flower of a healthy, vigorous stock of men in lowly life, which flourished for centuries, unknown to the world, in the quiet seclusion of a country parish in the county of Perth. The Croils, or Croyls, for so his forefathers used to spell their name, were inhabitants of the parish of Cargill for a period of at least two centuries. On examining the baptismal register of the parish, James was able to trace his parentage backwards in a direct line to about the middle of the seventeenth century. Here, unfortunately, the register comes to an end, and he was able to learn no more. Enough, however, remains to indicate that the Croils were a race of patient, plodding men, whose motto might well have been " Steady, aye steady."

For several generations the Croils were inhabitants of the small crofting village of Little Whitefield, in the parish of Cargill. This village contained only some eight or ten houses, whose tenants had about a hundred or a hundred and fifty acres of the surrounding land divided among them as crofts. Here Croll's father, David, son of Alexander Croil, was born in March 1781. Like his forefathers, he clung to his native soil. He learned the trade of a stonemason, and seems to have succeeded in securing for himself a house and croft in his native village only at a somewhat advanced period of his life. At all events, it was not till he had reached the mature age of thirty-seven that he ventured to enter upon married life. His wife, Janet, youngest daughter of James Ellis, of Elgin, was born in that city in 1781. She left Moray-shire for Perth during the early part of the present century; and, about the latter end of the year 1818, she was married to David Croil, who was of the same age as herself.

Croll's parents were both distinguished by the possession of great force of character and high intelligence. In some respects, however, they differed widely from one another. His mother was a woman of much native shrewdness, keen powers of observation, and great firmness of purpose. In the ordinary affairs of life she displayed no small amount of that remarkable commodity, usually termed " common sense," which generally indicates a well balanced mind and the power to do well in the battle of life. His father was a man of a deeply religious nature, warmly attached by both sympathy and conviction to the Independent or Congregational Church, whose members enjoyed a high reputation in the beginning of this century for their earnestness of purpose and purity of character. Endowed with considerable intellectual power, he was more inclined to a quietly meditative than to a busy, pushing life. Strictly conscientious in all things, he was also keenly sensitive by nature, and apt to be too easily troubled by the cares of life. His high moral character and amiable disposition secured for him the friendship and esteem of all who knew him. He was highly respected throughout the district in which he worked, and his children were always proud to tell, when asked, who their father was, as the mention of his name generally procured for them a friendly smile and the encouraging remark, " I hope that, when you grow up, you will be as good a man as your father."

The family of David Croil consisted of four sons, of whom James was the second. Alexander, the eldest, was born on the 29th of November 1819. He seems to have been a boy of much promise, able and willing to assist his younger brothers in the preparation of their lessons; and his death, which took place when he was about ten years old, threw a deep shadow over the family life. The parents felt the blow severely, especially the father, who never afterwards regained his usual vivacity of spirits. David, the third son, was born on the 23rd of April 1822. In infancy he was believed to have fallen from the arms of a girl who was nursing him. This accident brought on a curvature of the spine and general debility, so great that, although he lived to the age of fifty-four, he was never able to leave the shelter of the home circle and fight an independent battle with the world. William, the youngest of the family, was born on the 25th of February 1826 and died in infancy.

James, the second son of David and Janet Croil, was born at Little Whitefield, as already stated, on the 2nd of January 1821. Of his earliest years we know nothing beyond a few characteristic incidents which he has narrated in his autobiographical sketch. Even in infancy a certain delicacy of constitution seems to have become manifest; but, at the same time, some of his remarkable powers of mind were strikingly displayed. He could hardly have been more than eighteen months old when his brother David was baptized. His father was then a member of the Congregational Church in Perth; and the pastor, the Rev. Wm. Orme (afterwards of Camberwell, London), came out to Little Whitefield to perform the ceremony. Availing himself of the opportunity afforded by his visit, the minister conducted a religious service in the open air for the benefit of the villagers. Open-air services of this kind formed a very special feature in the ecclesiastical life of Scotland at this time. In connection with the Presbyterian Churches, established and non-established, there was usually a great gathering of the people in the open-air at sacramental seasons. Burns has immortalised these in his strikingly forcible satire, "The Holy Fair." During the early part of the century, however, a considerable revival of religion was awakened in the people of Scotland, by the itinerant preaching services of Rowland Hill and the brothers Haldane; and this was largely furthered and developed by the ministers of the Congregational or Independent Church. They regarded it as an important part of their work to make preaching tours throughout the country, to hold out-door services as opportunity was given, and to conduct Sabbath schools for the religious instruction of the young.

The Rev. William Orme was a rather remarkable man among them. It is a curious coincidence that, like Croll (as we shall see), he had served an apprenticeship as a wheelwright in the Grassmarket of Edinburgh. This occupation he only quitted in the month of October 1805, in his nineteenth year, to join Mr. Haldane's Academy, under the tuition of Mr. George Cowie, in preparation for the work of the ministry. Having completed his curriculum there, he was, in March 1807, called to the pastorate of the Congregational Church in Perth, where he laboured for seventeen years, only leaving the city when he accepted a call to a church in Camberwell,

London.   Soon after he went to Camberwell he led the English Dissenters in their agitation for the repeal of the odious and obnoxious " Test and Corporation Acts," in which he was successful.   He was a man of considerable intellectual ability, much energy and decision of character, while he also possessed the power of ready tongue and pen.   He wrote lives of Owen and Baxter, as also a copious and elaborate *Bibliotheca Biblica*, which showed extensive reading, great industry, and high attainments as a writer.   He also wrote the life of Kiffin, a Baptist minister in London, *Memoirs of John Urquhart*, an *Argument for the Weekly Observance of the Lord's Supper*, *Discourses on the Work of the Holy Spirit*, a *Catechism on the Constitution and Ordinances of the Kingdom of Christ*, and various articles for the magazines.

A contemporary says that long before his introduction to the metropolis, Mr. Orme had risen to high and distinguished eminence as an able preacher of the New Covenant ; and we have learned that in Perth he was considered one of the ablest and most popular ministers of his time.   He would therefore, no doubt, on a visit to a small hamlet like Little Whitefield, create considerable excitement in the neighbourhood.   His visit would be an event in the place ; and people would, doubtless, be gathered together in large numbers from the surrounding district to hear him preach.

Little James Croll was present at the service conducted by Mr. Orme, and the whole scene was so vividly impressed upon his mind that, even to his latest years, he retained a most distinct recollection of the interesting ceremony.   Other striking incidents of the first three years of his life were similarly treasured up in memory,—among them the stirring events of the day when the family removed from his earliest home, while, of the years subsequent to these, his mental record was singularly regular and complete, including every important incident in the history of himself and his family.   The remarkable power of accurate observation, thus early

4

displayed and afterwards developed by Croll, he seems to have inherited from his mother. The tenacious memory, from which nothing which interested him ever passed away, came from his father, whose recollections of the past went back to within two years of his own birth.

The first three years of Croll's life passed quietly away in the little hamlet, where his forefathers had lived for several generations. Then there came a change. In the early part of the present century the landed proprietors of Scotland were attacked by the mania for large farms. In many districts crofting villages were swept away to make room for a new style of agriculture; and the old inhabitants were turned adrift to shift for themselves as best they could. Among the old-fashioned hamlets thus abolished, to prepare for the formation of extensive farms, was Little Whitefield. In this case, however, the owner of the ground, Lord Willoughby, evinced a kindly sympathy with his humble tenants, and decided, in their interest, to set apart two pieces of land for feuing purposes: the first, a stretch of waste land, about a mile to the south of Little Whitefield, now known as Wolfhill; the second, a bit of ground lying three miles to the north, now called Burreltown. David Croll took a feu in the former district, erected on it a dwelling-house and other buildings necessary for a crofter, and then, in 1824, removed with his family to their new home. Availing himself of the permission granted to the feuars in the new village, to reclaim a part of the waste ground in the vicinity, he employed himself in this work during the time which he could spare from his labours as a stonemason; and by and by, having succeeded in bringing some four or five acres into fairly good condition, he felt himself restored to his former position.

Having established himself with his wife and children in the new home at Wolfhill, David Croll resumed the even tenor of his humble, industrious life. Himself a highly thoughtful man, he had his own views on the early education of the young. It seemed to him that the physical system ought to be allowed a considerable period of natural, healthy development, before the work of direct mental training was begun. Accordingly, James was granted three or four more years of careless ease, in which no thought of lessons ever disturbed his dreams. At length, when it seemed high time that he should enter upon the usual routine of school life, an unexpected difficulty presented itself. He had begun to suffer from a somewhat troublesome pain on the top or about the opening of his head. He was thus unable to remain with uncovered head for any length of time, except in the very heat of summer; and as he could not on any account be persuaded to sit beside his uncovered companions with a cap on his head, his parents were reluctantly compelled to keep him at home and give him private lessons. Thus it happened that his first teacher was his father, who was at times assisted by his eldest son, a lad but two years the senior of his pupil. From time to time James also received a private lesson from the master of the little village school; and so, amid many difficulties, he acquired the elements of reading and writing. Even the schoolmaster, who assisted the father and brother in the work of teaching the young philosopher, seems to have been but very imperfectly qualified for his task; he was an elderly man who had once occupied a more lucrative position in the world but had latterly been compelled, through reverse of fortune, to eke out a scanty livelihood by giving lessons to a few boys in the quiet village of Wolfhill. After about two years of somewhat mixed and fragmentary instruction at home, James was sent, for a short time, to the parish school of Cargill, a mile and a half distant from his home; and by and by he was removed to a voluntary school in the village of Guildtown, about two miles west of Wolfhill. The master here, unfortunately, was a rough, pompous, and tyrannical man, who fully succeeded in inspiring his pupils with a thorough detestation of school and all that was connected with it. It must surely have been of him that Croll, in after years, told the following absurdly ludicrous story:—"One day the 'dominie' was giving the boys their usual Bible lesson, when he suddenly asked the question 'Which of all the prophets, in your opinion, most resembled the Apostle Paul?' Each of the lads, in turn, gave the answer which seemed to him the most appropriate. At last the teacher approached a boy who generally sat at the foot of the class, and never, in any case, was able to rise more than one or two places higher. On this occasion, however, he seemed unusually anxious to be heard; and, when the question was put to him, he at once answered, 'It's yer ainsel, sir.' The astonishment of his comrades may be imagined; but what must have been their feelings when the master calmly replied 'That's a good boy; you go up to the top of the class for that'?" That a man of whom such a story could be related should have been accepted as an instructor of youth in a village but a few miles distant from the city of Perth, seems hardly credible in these days. That he failed to excite any enthusiasm for learning even in the mind of young Croll can excite no surprise. Fortunately for the district, he was soon replaced by Mr. Keiller, a much more kindly and intelligent man, whose work was naturally attended by more satisfactory results. James Croll, however, enjoyed but little of his good offices. He was now (1834) thirteen years of age; and, after some eight or nine months under the new teacher, he left school finally, to enter upon other work.

Croll's school days, taken altogether, extended over a period of about six years; but there were blank spaces in this period, his teachers were too frequently changed, and, as we all know, too many masters spoil the lad. His training seems to have been wholly confined to the three R's; and, even within these narrow limits, the work was but poorly done. The eager, active intellect of the boy was never roused by his early teachers, his interest was never stirred by anything they presented to his view. Bright and intelligent, full of fun and frolic, he was left to spend his energy on out-of-doors schemes and occupations. In some respects, in view of a certain delicacy of constitution which had already appeared, we may regard this as a bit of good fortune. To the surprise and disappointment of his father, he was (he himself tells us) a rather dull scholar, scarcely up to the average of boys of the same age in the matter of getting up lessons quickly and correctly. He failed to acquire an accurate style of reading; and by no amount of labour could he succeed in learning to spell even moderately well. For him the teacher (so called) was a mere taskmaster, the lessons the labour of a bondsman, like the making of bricks without straw. His real teachers were to be found outside the village schoolroom, the forces which stirred his youthful intellect were to speed from a far distance. In due season they drew near, they acted with quickening power, they presented the wonders of science in all their beauty and charm, they aroused in the boy a passionate desire for the higher education; but, alas! they did so only as the unbending force of circumstances was compelling him to enter upon a lowly lot in active life.

Croll's father was not merely a working stonemason; he was also a crofter, holding some four or five acres of land, the cultivation of which involved a considerable amount of labour. During the greater part of the year he followed the work of his trade, which carried him to many different places at a greater or less distance from home. The lot of a mason in these times in Scotland was rather a hard one. Carlyle, writing of his father and a companion, both of whom were masons, says: " The two 'slung their tools' (mallets and irons hung in two equipoised masses on the shoulders) and crossed the hills into Nithsdale to Auldgarth, where a bridge was building. This was my father's most foreign adventure. He never again, or before, saw anything so new; or, except when he came to Craigenputtock on visits, so distant. He loved to speak of it. That talking day we had together I made him tell it me all over again from the beginning, as a whole, for the first time. He was a 'hewer,' and had some few pence a day. He could describe with the lucidest distinctness how the whole work went on, and 'headers' and 'closers' solidly massed together made an impregnable pile."[1] "A noble craft it is, that of a mason; a good building will last longer than most books, than one book of a million. I have a dim picture of him (my father) in his little world. In summer season diligently, cheerfully labouring with trowel and hammer, amused by grave talk and grave humour with the doers of the craft. Building, walling, is an operation that beyond most other ones requires incessant consideration,—even new invention." But for all this, as we have been told, they only earned a few pence a day. In the "dear years" (1799 and 1800), says Carlyle, "when the oatmeal was as high as ten shillings a stone, he had noticed the labourers (I have heard him tell) retire each separately to a brook and there drink instead of dining, without complaint, anxious only to hide it."[2]

The mere possession of the croft evinced a strong desire to improve the condition of the stonemason and his family. The little farm, if well worked, was sure to add considerably to the comforts of the household, but it also added greatly to the toils of the hard-working parents. When we consider that those four or five acres had first to be reclaimed from a state of bog or moorland waste, and by years of unceasing hard labour—breaking up, draining, and manuring—brought into a state of cultivation and rendered really productive, we cannot but wonder that, in conjunction with the severe daily toil of a stonemason, Croll's father was able to accomplish such a work at all. Yet, like many other hard-headed and hard-handed Scotchmen, he, along with his wife and family, did so. The wife and children, of course, lent a helping and at times. The work of reclaiming could be carried

[1] *Rem* i. 45, 47, 48   [2] *Ibid.* i. 61.

on at any season of the year; but when the ground was brought into a state of cultivation, the labour of making it productive could be accomplished only at the appropriate seasons of the year. There was not sufficient work to occupy Croll throughout the year on his croft, and it would have been impossible for him in such a way to earn a competent sustenance for himself and his family. He therefore continued, as we have seen, to follow his occupation of stonemason, which often took him from home. The working of the croft was thus left mainly in the hands of his wife, who occasionally obtained from outside helpers such assistance as was indispensable. In ordinary circumstances, however, she required some regular assistance at home. Her eldest son, Alexander, had died some five years before the present date (1834), and James had for some time been engaged at intervals in bits of humble farm work. The position of the affairs of the family now demanded that he should devote himself regularly to this occupation; and, accordingly, with an aching heart, he left school, when not quite fourteen years of age, to enter upon his apprenticeship to the stern work of life.

CHAPTER II

INTELLECTUAL NEW BIRTH AND LIFE-EDUCATION

CROLL'S early teachers did nothing in the way of educating the boy; and the few books in his father's possession were by no means such as to attract his attention or awaken in him any intellectual interest. Thus, up to the age of about eleven and a half years, he evinced no taste for reading, and gave absolutely no promise of his future career. His intellectual new birth had not yet taken place. That event, however, was near at hand. In the beginning of April 1832, when he was on a visit to the city of Perth, he paused one day to look into the window of a bookseller, where some of the latest productions of the press were displayed. His attention was arrested by the illustrations of a little periodical paper, chiefly, perhaps, by the picture of a brown bear walking on his hind legs along a tree which crossed a river, and carrying a dead horse in his fore paws. He entered the shop and purchased the first number of the *Penny Magazine*, which had just been established by " The Society for the Diffusion of Useful Knowledge" for the purpose of acting, like the stage-coach, " as a means of convenience and enjoyment to the people at large." Carrying his treasure home, the country boy found, in the eight large pages of the little magazine, what to him was truly a feast of reason, a feast which in him produced a flow of soul. Here he found a historical article on Charing Cross, London; articles geographical, historical, and social, on Van Diemen's Land and Poland; brief biographical sketches of René Descartes, mathematician

and metaphysician, and of Dr. William Harvey, the dis-
coverer of the circulation of the blood; an outline of the
life of the Rev. George Crabbe, with a poetical extract
from his *Parish Register* on Isaac Ashford, whom he
describes as "a noble peasant, a wise good man, contented to be poor"; accounts of the Wapiti (deer) and
the bear in the Zoological Gardens; a quaint sermon on
malt, and an article on the antiquity of beer; and, lastly,
a few columns of miscellanea. The boy perused with
ever deepening interest the pages of the little magazine,
in which a new world seemed to be opening up to his
view. He purchased the following numbers of the new
periodical regularly as they appeared, and became a
diligent student of its contents. In this way he became
acquainted with the life story of men of many lands and
ages who had risen to eminence in all departments of
life; he learned something of the great works of art,
ancient and modern, in painting, sculpture, and architec-
ture, as well as of historically interesting antiquities
of a different order; he gained some insight into many
striking features of natural history, and he was at times
carried away by romantic narratives of travel and adventure; while, at the same time, he had presented to his
mind, in simple and attractive style, the elementary
principles of language and numbers, along with well
established facts in statistics and economy. The contents of the *Penny Magazine* were, in short, encyclopædic;
and, through its volumes, young Croll gained his first
notions both of natural science and of philosophy, of
which he was afterwards to become so distinguished a
student. So highly did he appreciate the benefits he
had received from it, that, in later years, he took the
trouble of procuring several odd volumes of the work,
that he might be the possessor of a complete copy of the
magazine from its first number down to its last.

Croll had now entered on a new epoch in his life; his
intellectual interest had been aroused; and he had made
a beginning in the great work of self-education. There

arose within him a great longing for a better training
than he was receiving at the village school; but, alas!
the means wherewithal were not to be found. He felt,
however, that at any cost he must continue not only
to read, but still more to extend his course. In the
pages of his first tutor he had perused occasional notices
of important works in various departments of literature
and science; and as the magazine articles had only
whetted his appetite, he determined to lay aside his
occasional pence of pocket-money, and devote them to
the purchase of books.

Among the first of the volumes which he succeeded
in obtaining was *The Christian Philosopher; or, The
Connection of Science and Philosophy with Religion*, by
Dr. Thomas Dick. This work, although very far from
being a " book for boys," proved very valuable to our
young student in the way of stimulating his interest in
lofty subjects of thought, extending his views of the
world in which we live, and developing all his recently
awakened powers of mind. The object of the author
was to illustrate the harmony which subsists between
the system of nature and the system of revelation, and
to show that the manifestation of God in the material
universe ought to be blended with our views of the facts
and doctrines recorded in the volume of inspiration. In
his first volume he treats of the natural attributes of the
Deity in their relation to religion; he presents his readers
with a rich variety of phenomena drawn from many fields
of science in illustration of the omnipotence, wisdom, and
goodness of God; and he gives a cursory but careful view
of natural history, geography, geology, and astronomy in
their relation to religion and Christian theology. In the
second volume he deals in like fashion with natural philosophy, chemistry, anatomy, physiology, and the inven-
tions of human art; he treats of various scriptural facts
and doctrines which may be illustrated from the system
of nature; and he urges the advantages to be derived
from an enlarged study of science in connection with

philosophy. The effect at first produced on the mind
of young Croll by his plunge into this view of science,
philosophy, and philosophic facts and reasonings may be
more easily imagined than described. He was utterly
bewildered by the novelty and grandeur of the conceptions presented to his mind in almost measureless number
and variety. With dauntless energy and tenacity of
purpose, however, unaided by friend or teacher, he pursued his solitary path through the teeming pages of Dick's
work, slowly mastering facts and reasonings, till order,
simplicity, and beauty became manifest in what had at
first seemed a mere chaos of perplexity and confusion;
and now his amazement and bewilderment gave place to
admiration and delight. Strange to say, what chiefly
charmed the boy, even in his earliest scientific reading,
was not the miscellaneous array of striking phenomena
in all departments of nature drawn up before him for
inspection, but the general laws or principles which underlay these phenomena, and gave them order and beauty.
Any novel phenomenon which was presented to his mind
suggested irresistibly the question How? and the statement of the general law to which this phenomenon could
be referred was usually followed by another How? Croll
could find no rest for his mind except in fundamental
principles. Thus physical astronomy (the only branch
of astronomy which he ever studied), while it deeply
interested him, failed to give him any real satisfaction
on his first acquaintance with it. He was ignorant of
the mathematical and mechanical principles on which it
depends.

Croll accordingly determined to set about the study
of science in systematic fashion, impelled by the difficulties
he had found in his perusal of Dick's *Christian Philosopher*,
of which he had probably read only the first volume.
He purchased one or two books which seemed likely to
prove helpful to him, and among them was Joyce's
Scientific Dialogues. In this valuable work, which for
many years aided greatly in extending a knowledge of

physical science among the young, he found a real treasure. An exposition of the first principles of experimental philosophy prepared for the instruction and entertainment of young people, it was drawn up in the form of conversations between a father and his children, and carefully adapted to the capacities of those of ten or eleven years of age. To the youth who had fearlessly, and with some success, attacked the grim pages of Dick's bulky, close-wrought volumes, those of Joyce's slenderer work promised a speedy and triumphant victory. He positively revelled in the perusal of the book. The romance of science was that which early fascinated his mind and kindled his imagination. Swiftly laying hold of the mass of interesting facts laid out before him, he passed with avidity to the mastery of the general principles which underlay them all and gave them meaning and value in his view. To the details of the construction of philosophical instruments, such as the air-pump or the electrical machine, he paid little or no attention, except in so far as they illustrated the laws of pneumatics or electricity according to which these instruments operated. The details excited his interest only for a moment; as soon as the general laws or principles were firmly grasped, they ceased to charm, and largely passed away from his mind. The thorough mastery of principles to which he set himself, and by means of which he was enabled easily to recall facts and details when necessary, gave the young student an enormous advantage in the prosecution of his work. He was able to advance by leaps and bounds without the assistance of any friend or teacher, where the progress of others who enjoy such assistance is usually very slow. In this way, in the course of some four or five years from the day on which he first opened the *Penny Magazine*, namely, by the time he was about sixteen years old, he had gained a pretty tolerable knowledge of the general principles of mechanics, pneumatics, hydrostatics, heat, light, electricity, and magnetism.

Two very important and, to most people, very interesting branches of science utterly failed to attract young Croll. The fact that they are so largely sciences of observation and experiment, which gives them their interest in the minds of most people, was the means of repelling him. For chemistry and geology, "more particularly the latter," he had no relish. They appeared to him to be so largely made up of mere facts and details, so deficient in rational principles; they seemed to be so lacking in the philosophic method and material which were to him as the very breath of life, that he positively shrank from them. Had any one told him, he says, in his early years, that he would one day become a professional geologist, he would have regarded the statement as incredible. In fact, it was largely by what men call *accident*, more by the constraint of others than by his own personal choice, that in later years he entered the office of the Geological Survey. If we except one department of geology, to which we shall by and by have occasion to refer, it was almost the only science to the study of which he never devoted a single day. He never became, never cared to become, a geologist, in the ordinary sense of the term, even although he became a member of the Geological Survey staff. Nevertheless, his acceptance of a post on that staff proved of immense advantage to him in the pursuit of the climatological studies which made him famous, as it afforded him a comparatively easy means of gaining an acquaintance with geological phenomena, phenomena of which, but for that appointment, he would most probably have remained ignorant; and without the knowledge of which his important work would have been but very imperfectly accomplished.

Thus, in the quiet seclusion of the little village of Wolfhill, passed away the years of Croll's boyhood. They were formative years; by the sacred influences of his parents' pious home, his naturally religious and meditative soul was unconsciously educated; while, from the pages of the *Penny Magazine*, Dick's *Christian Philosopher*, Joyce's *Scientific Dialogues*, and a few other books to which he was mysteriously guided, he received intellectual impressions and impulses from the influence of which he never escaped. His mental being was stirred to its very depths by the grandeur of the conceptions presented to him in these works; and he received from them an impetus towards the pursuit of truth in natural science and in mental philosophy which remained with him to the end.[1] Indeed, no grand physical conceptions which he ever acquired in later years made such an impression on his mind as those of this early date; excepting, perhaps, those relating to the modern science of energy,—its transformation and its conservation, and to the dynamical theory and the mechanical equivalent of heat. Thus the moral character of the man was determined, his intellectual bent was assigned, and his whole course in life was largely influenced.

For a period of nearly three years, from the age of about fourteen, he was almost wholly engaged during the daytime in the agricultural labour demanded by the culture of his father's croft.

[1] See solitary musing, described on p. 18.

CHAPTER III

CHOICE OF A TRADE

AFTER Croll had been labouring on the croft for two or three years, it became evident to his father and mother, as well as to himself, that some occupation better than that of a crofter must be found for him. What that occupation should be proved a perplexing question to all. Croll himself had, since the "reading fit" came on him, become imbued with an ardent thirst for knowledge and a desire for more education. He had been quietly but perseveringly trying to satisfy the thirst and the desire, and had succeeded only in enormously stimulating them. Accordingly, now, when about to take his first step into the world, he felt the strongest desire to receive the benefit of a university education. The satisfaction of this desire unfortunately proved altogether impossible. His father was too poor to support the lad during the usual four years of a university curriculum, and he had no relations rich enough to render any assistance. In those days the bursaries open to poor but promising students at our Scottish Universities were neither very numerous nor very large; but even had they been more numerous, Croll had not proved himself one of those brilliant boys who, by diligent study at the parish school, have always, in Scotland, been able to enjoy a university education at very small cost to parents or friends. The nearest university was St. Andrews, which was about forty miles distant from Wolfhill; and although several bursaries are annually awarded there to clever lads, these were altogether beyond the reach of Croll, who had enjoyed no systematic training in even the elements of mathematics or the Latin or Greek languages. His longing desire for a university education had thus to be stifled, and the project given up as impracticable and unattainable. What else, then, could the lad do? He had no special aptitude or desire for any particular trade; but to trade he must go, since his irregular and imperfect education shut him out from the professions. After pondering anxiously over the matter for several days and consulting his friends, he came to the conclusion that, as he had made some study of the theory of mechanics, he might find the work of a millwright one in which his study would be of some service to him. Accordingly, it was resolved that he should be apprenticed to a millwright; and in the village of Collace he entered upon this trade. He himself says little of the experiences of the years of his apprenticeship; and we have not been able to ascertain anything further than what is recorded in the autobiography.

On the completion of his apprenticeship, he left Collace and went to work as a journeyman with the firm of Martin & Robertson, millwrights at Banchory, Coupar-Angus. The business of this firm was chiefly that of making and repairing threshing-mills throughout the " Howe " of Strathmore and the surrounding districts. They usually employed some four or five men at this work, whose wages were by no means large, about eight shillings per week together with food, which was usually of the poorest description possible. The repairs on the corn-saw and threshing-mills had usually to be executed at the different farms where the mills were erected; and this, of course, caused the men to be constantly shifting about from place to place, so that they scarcely ever spent more than a day or two at one place. In those days there were no railways in the Howe of Strathmore; and the men were frequently compelled to walk long distances on foot,—sometimes of thirty or forty miles a day,—in order to fulfil their engagements. With his usual dry humour Croll says quietly, " It was on the whole rather a rough life." The millwright was looked on as somewhat of the nature of a tramp ; and he had generally to rest in the ploughman's " bothy," which, in those days, was a very rough outhouse belonging to the farm, consisting of little more than the four bare walls and containing several beds, a table, and a few chairs or forms. When the bothy was full, the poor millwright had to betake himself to the barn or the stable-loft above the horses, where he had to bury himself under the clothes, generally a few sacks, to protect himself from the rats.

Croll endured these hardships very patiently for a period of some five or six years ; but he gradually came to see that this trade was wholly unsuited to the development of either his mind or his body. His experiences during this period, however, did not fail to leave their marks upon his constitution. Long after, in consequence of the excessively long walks he had to perform, his feet were so grown over with corns, that he was obliged to cut holes in his shoes, and allow the corns to grow out without cutting or paring them. During all these years of trial, Croll performed his arduous duties without a grumble, while, according to the testimony of those who knew him then, "his moral character and daily deportment were most exemplary and in every way commendable." The Rev. Mr. Bruce, Free Church minister, Rhynie, writes of him at this period, " I never heard a complaint brought against him by any one. But, on the contrary, everybody spoke well of him, and had the highest respect for him. To me, who was a few years his junior, there always seemed something so modest and unaffected about him which naturally drew my affections towards him and reverence for him."

Croll abandoned the millwright trade when about twenty-two years of age, and returned to the village of

5

Collace for a season. He had probably saved a little money out of his hard-earned wages, for we find that, the insatiable craving for education having attacked him again, he went to the parish school of St. Martins for a winter to study algebra. The sight of a grown-up, grave-looking working man attending the parish school for "counting," as the schoolboys called it, was a source of wonder and amusement to the lads. Yet cases like this were to be seen in many of the better schools in Scotland, both in town and country, and the younger pupils were rarely rude to such men. During this winter, doubtless, Croll lent a helping hand to his parents in the working of the croft, and made himself generally useful at home. At the opening of the summer, however, he was obliged to resume work, as his little hoard of savings had been almost wholly exhausted, and he had again to earn his livelihood. He accordingly sought and obtained employment as a joiner. His new trade he readily learned so well as to become a very efficient tradesman, and he found it much more suited to his taste, as he did not require to travel from place to place so much, while the life in general was by no means so hard.

The first big job on which Croll was engaged as a joiner was the erection of the Free Church at Kinrossie, in the parish of Collace, of which the Rev. Andrew A. Bonar (afterwards D.D., of Glasgow) was then minister. Collace was some two or three miles distant from Wolf-hill; the joiners began work at 6 A.M. and ceased about 6 P.M.; and as it seemed too much for the young man, with already injured feet, to do a hard day's work and walk such a distance both morning and evening, Croll's father thought he should reside at Collace. The kindly old man accordingly called on some of his friends in Collace with this object in view, and one of them agreed " to make way for him among the young folks." This villager is still alive, and writes:

" So James came next morning, and continued with

us all the time the building was going on. In a few days after this, Mr. Andrew Bonar, now Dr. Bonar of Finniston, who was our minister, then called at our house in his ordinary course, and in course of ordinary conversation he says, 'By the bye, haven't you James Croll staying with you.' We said we had. 'Then,' said he, 'how do you get on with James?' I said, 'Remarkably well; I think he is one of the nicest young men I have ever met with.' 'But,' says Mr. Bonar, 'how do you get on with him in your conversations?' I said, 'Remarkably well, so far as I can follow him, but sometimes, when I think the subject of conversation is made clear enough, and no more can be made of it, James is not satisfied; he has some ulterior view—something beyond in his eye that I am not able to follow him.' Mr. Bonar laughed most heartily and said, 'I don't wonder at it, Andrew, I don't wonder at it. Do you know that James has a very striking metaphysical cast of mind?'"

The new Free Church was the church being erected at the time of the Disruption in 1843. It appears that Mr. Bonar, an able and zealous minister, was then in the habit of gathering together a number of grown-up young men in his house on the Sunday evenings, after the services of the day were over, for spiritual instruction. Croll took advantage of this class, and speedily attracted the attention of the minister, who formed a high opinion of him. Writing in 1891, Dr. Bonar says: "It is long since I met James Croll, though in earlier days I knew him well. He lived at that time in the village of Wolfhill, parish of Cargill, not far from where my lot was cast. He was known among us as a young disciple who showed a great inclination to philosophical study, and he was much esteemed."

After the Free Church at Kinrossie was completed, there happened to be a scarcity of building work in the neighbourhood, and in the summer of 1844, Croll removed to Glasgow, where he soon found employment. He remained in Glasgow for only a few months, removing then to Paisley, where he stayed for about a year. He liked this place and his employment. About this time a controversy arose in theological circles between Calvinists and Arminians. Croll took a deep interest in this controversy, and joined the Arminians, then called Morisonians after Dr. Morison, who was the leader of the new movement. He attached himself to a number of the followers of Dr. Morison, who were endeavouring to found a church in Paisley under the preaching first of Mr., afterwards Dr., Landels, now of Edinburgh, and then of the Rev. Mr. A. M. Wilson, afterwards of Bathgate. He took a warm interest in the formation of this church, and was elected a deacon, but he did not enter upon office, as he was obliged to leave the town before he was called upon to act.

When Croll was working at his trade in Paisley, in the spring of 1846, the elbow joint of his left arm became so seriously inflamed, that he felt compelled to consult his medical adviser, who told him that he must abandon his trade as a joiner, and adopt some easier occupation, which would not necessitate so much physical exertion. It appears that this ailment had its origin in a boil, which appeared on his arm when he was a boy of about ten or eleven. Unfortunately, it was accidentally knocked against the corner of a door, and it proved very troublesome both during the healing up and afterwards, and continued to afflict him more or less every spring for several years. There was nothing for it but to return home and rest for a season, consider his position, and decide what should be done in the future. Accordingly, he left Paisley, and returned to his father's house at Wolfhill. There he remained for some time, reading and studying diligently, till the arm got better; but unfortunately it never recovered sufficiently to allow him to use it freely, as the joint ultimately ossified, and Croll suffered ever afterwards from a stiff elbow.

He was now in a greater dilemma than ever. The joiner business, or, indeed, any kind of trade, was out of the question. He had neither the education nor the training to fit him for a clerkship, and, moreover, he had no aptitude or inclination for such an occupation. He thought he might get some kind of employment in the tea trade; and accordingly one day walked to the city of Perth, a distance of about eight miles, to make inquiries. The story of his selection and adoption of this trade is so romantic and interesting, that, although it involves repetition, it can be told only in his own words: "Musing over the matter, as I approached the city by the bridge, I observed a man distributing small handbills to the passers-by. All in a moment it struck me that if these bills should relate to the tea trade, I would be guided by this, and would go to the shop to which they referred; at least, before trying any other. What could induce me to come to a conclusion so apparently absurd and incautious, I cannot tell. Strange are the ways of Providence! for had it not been for that decision, in all probability, my future course in life would have been very different from what it actually turned out to be. On coming up to the man, I found the bills related to a tea and coffee warehouse which had recently been opened in the High Street of Perth. Guided by the bill, I went direct to the shop, and found the proprietor to be an agreeable and intelligent person. After talking over various matters, I then told him what I had been think-ing about. He agreed with me that I might manage to make a comfortable livelihood by selling tea; and that I might push the sale by going into the country. I accord-ingly got a small stock and commenced operations. I soon found, however, that the attempt to push a sale in the country was a rather disagreeable job for me, and I resolved to give it up. The merchant whom I had visited—Mr. David Irons, who afterwards proved to be one of the kindest friends I have ever met with in life—now proposed to me that I might try and open a shop for myself in some suitable town, where I might be likely to succeed. Unfortunately I had not the means for any such undertaking; but he, in the most kindly manner, offered to assist me. He agreed to give me a stock to commence with, and that I should repay him in regular instalments as it was sold; and that he would in this way keep up my stock. I need hardly say that an offer so generous was readily accepted. As it was now about the end of the harvest season, my friend suggested that I might come to Perth for the winter, and learn the mechanical art of weighing and parcelling up the tea, serving over the counter, and all the usual routine of shop work. I accordingly came in, and before the winter was over, I became a thoroughly proficient shopkeeper."

Croll, as " a thoroughly proficient shopkeeper, learned in the mechanical art of weighing and parcelling up the tea, serving over the counter, and all the routine of shop work," is a dream which existed only as a picture in his own imagination, arising largely out of gratitude for a kind act, and thankfulness for a tranquil period of his life. The reality was very different from the picture. The primary qualification for a shopkeeper is an affable, agreeable, and, as some would say, almost obsequious manner. Croll had, to the day of his death, a modest, shy, dry, and almost speechless manner, except on occasions when he was drawn out by congenial conversation among real friends. A second requisite is an active and attractive appearance, alertness and energy of body. Croll was heavy and ungainly in appearance, solid, sound as a rock, true as steel, but somewhat slow and awkward in manner and appearance. A third requisite is adroitness in " serving over the counter." Croll never was very adroit either in mind or body, and could and did serve only with his natural reserve and shyness. A fourth requisite is rapidity and neatness in the mechanical art of weighing and parcelling up the tea, and in the general routine of shop work. Croll never was either rapid or neat in any mechanical work he performed; and with his hands and arms trained only to the hard work of a millwright or joiner, as well as the awkwardness and inaptitude caused by the weakness and stiffness of his elbow, it can easily be seen that he could not be a proficient by any means in the "mechanical art of weighing and parcelling up the tea." His appearance behind the counter is well described by an eye-witness: "It was something altogether extraordinary to see the man, with his large head, massive forehead, and kindly countenance, with his heavy form of body, hard horny hands and stiff arm, standing behind the counter of a tea-shop. One is accustomed to see rather a small thin man with thin nimble fingers and active arms discharging this duty; and no one, even the most casual observer, could see Croll in the character of shopkeeper at this time without knowing that he was not a shopkeeper to the manner born, and that he was evidently in a new sphere."

During the time he was in Perth, however, he was happy. His friend, Mr. David Irons, was a kind, intelligent, well-read man, who took a deep interest in him, had many conversations with him on religious matters, and encouraged him in all that pertained to his spiritual and temporal welfare. As he had gone to Perth only to learn the tea trade, it now became necessary to fix on a place in which he might begin business. After looking about a while, he thought that there was an opening in Elgin for a tea merchant. Accordingly, that place was fixed upon, and he went north in the spring of 1847, and opened a tea-shop there. For a time he was comparatively successful in business, and liked the place and the people well. Instead, however, of developing the social side of his life, and making friends with the people, he became a hard philosophical student. He got hold of the great work of Jonathan Edwards, on the Freedom of the Will, which he read and re-read, both in season and out of season. Tappan's book he also tackled; but, like many other readers of this work, he was greatly disappointed. He found, in common with most philosophical students, that Tappan missed the point of

Edwards' argument altogether, and failed to grapple with the real difficulty of the problem. He never discovered any satisfactory answer to Edwards' argument, and "became convinced that some moderate form of Calvinism was nearest the truth, not only of philosophy, but also of Scripture."

Here, in Elgin, it was that Croll first formed the opinion which he matured and developed at intervals from that time to his death, namely, that "the entire universe is a process of determinations; but not of determinations occurring at random. There are a unity, a plan, and a purpose pervading the whole which imply thought and intelligence." Again and again he returned to this thought, he brooded over it, and wrote upon it in magazines and pamphlets, till it reached its final form in his last work.

On the 11th of September 1848, he was married to Isabella, second daughter of Mr. John Macdonald, Forres. It is a curious coincidence that Croll's mother belonged to Elgin, and his wife to the immediately adjoining town of Forres. In his own simple, manly way, he writes briefly on his married life, saying only: "The union has proved a happy one. She has been the sharer of my joys, sorrows, and trials (and these have not been few) for the past forty years. Her care, economy, and kindly attention to my comfort during the years of comparative hardships through which we have passed, have cheered me on during all my trials and sorrows." Croll was a man of few words, but a better deserved, a truer tribute of gratitude and respect to the partner of his life, never was penned by any man.

Like many more bachelors in their solitude, Croll had formed a fond liking for the fragrant weed, and, for some time, indulged this taste to such an extent as to produce the inevitable result of excessive smoking—a dyspeptic affection. He tried to give up the habit several times, but failed. At last, getting one or two friends to join him, he made a written pledge, on the

29th of December 1849, to abandon the habit; and from that date up to the end, he adhered strictly to his pledge. This little incident gives the keynote to the character of the man. Nothing could deter him from the accomplishment of what he deliberately resolved upon and undertook. "I had a terrible struggle with the appetite. For two or three months I was in a state of partial stupor; and it was nearly three years before the craving for tobacco left me." But, having once set his hand to the plough, he scorned the very idea of turning back.

In this connection it may be mentioned that he had been a pledged abstainer from intoxicating liquor for several years. His parents had never been in the habit of using intoxicating liquors, which, indeed, were a luxury for which they had no need, no funds, and no inclination. Croll had, therefore, been practically an abstainer from infancy; but when he came to the years of maturity, he gave in his adhesion to total abstinence as a matter of principle. During the time he was in Elgin he acted as secretary of the Temperance Society there.

In the course of his philosophical and religious reading, Croll had become acquainted with the writings of the Rev. James (afterwards Dr.) Morison, of Kilmarnock; and, about the year 1848 he opened up a correspondence with this eminent theologian, which continued at intervals to the time of his death. A letter from Croll to Dr. Morison, dated 24th November 1849, gives a vivid glimpse of the man as he then was.

ELGIN, *24th November* 1849.

MR. MORISON—DEAR SIR,—I duly received your kind letter, and am much obliged to you for its contents, all the more so when I consider how little time you must have for so particular details such as it contains. You express at the end of your note a wish to know something concerning me. This I am most happy to do, though I am sure that, when you know it, it will be of little service to you. I am twenty-

eight years and married, but have no family. My
parents dwell near St. Martins, Perthshire. I was a
wright to trade, but four or five years ago I was
obliged to give up my trade on account of a sore arm,
and through the kindness of a few friends, particularly
Mr. John Lister, I was enabled to commence business
here about three years ago as a grocer. When young,
I got a good many years at school, but, I am sorry to say,
made little or no progress, having always had a perfect
hatred to school. My deficiency in spelling, writing,
grammar, has been a great loss to me in after years.
When I was about twelve years old, I happened to fall
in with a book upon theoretical astronomy which perfectly fascinated me, and in order to get a knowledge
of that subject, I commenced the study of mechanics
and mathematics, and pursued eagerly this subject for
six or seven years, as far as time would permit me, to
the neglect of everything else but what I was obliged
to do. But being brought under deep religious impressions, I abandoned them altogether, and afterwards
studiously avoided them, knowing the danger I was
then in of being led away by them if I commenced
again. I was brought to the truth under Mr. Bonar,
Collace, and about that time your works on the atone-
ment happened to come my way. The reasoning
contained in them was so forcible that I could not
resist it, and I became an advocate of your views, and
eagerly read all the books written on that subject by
you and others who were thus cast out. I was in
Paisley when the church was formed there, and left
that place a little after Mr. Wilson came. Some years
ago I fell in with Lord Kames on Liberty and Necessity,
and Edwards on the Will. That latter book perfectly
astonished me. I studied it over and over again, till I
got completely master of it. I saw that Calvinism was
a subject that was not so easily got rid of, which set me
in earnest to fathom the *mystery* how to get quit of
" awful necessity," in order to get a comprehensive view

of the subject. I commenced the study of the philosophy of mind, and read Brown, Reid, and some of D. Stewart on that subject; with Combe, Spurzheim, Smith, and others on the phrenological view of the subject. So, instead of having got satisfaction, I am in no hope that for years to come will I be so clear upon that subject as I would fain wish and expect, though I am perfectly satisfied that liberty is right. There is one comfort, however, that the doctrine of necessity (philosophical) is hid in mist and metaphysics, so that few can see it so as to believe it and act upon the belief. But I must stop, for I have by this time wearied you with what will be of little interest to you.—I am, dear sir, your obedient servant,

JAMES CROLL.

The arm to which Croll refers in this letter began about this time to give him more trouble. The elbow joint was again attacked by inflammation; the effect of which, on this occasion, was to completely destroy the joint and render it stiff and immovable. This was a sore trial to him; but it stopped further inflammation of the elbow or trouble with the arm, and he afterwards enjoyed better general health. This illness unfitted him for some time for attending properly to the business of his shop, in consequence of which the trade fell off, and he was never able to restore the business. He tried hard to regain his lost footing, but in vain; and after a while, finding that he was only losing money, he, in dread of falling into debt, realised his business, paid his debts, closed the shop, and left Elgin forthwith.

CHAPTER IV

RETURN TO PERTH IN 1850

IN the beginning of the summer of 1850, Croll, having left Elgin for good, returned to the city of Perth. He had not, however, quite regained health after his illness at Elgin, and it was a considerable time till he recovered so fully as to be able to do any manual work. At this time the effect of electricity and galvanism for medical purposes had begun to attract attention, and Croll now applied himself to the study of this subject. He had long ago studied electricity in its theoretical aspect, and was familiar with the principles upon which electrical machines were necessarily constructed. It was comparatively easy for him, therefore, to understand upon what principle an electric or galvanic battery must act. It was not so easy, however, for a disabled joiner or tea merchant to construct such a machine. Nothing possible, however, daunted Croll. Dire necessity drove him to do something to earn a livelihood for himself and his wife; and so he applied himself to the construction of induction apparatus. These machines proved thoroughly well made, complete in all respects, and well adapted to the end in view. The writer had one of them in his possession for several years, which he only parted with to Croll himself in later years; and as he subsequently found out, it was given away to a poor person who could not afford to buy one. He continued the making of these machines for some time; but, within the comparatively limited area of Perth and Dundee, the demand for them was very small, and soon became exhausted. With what he made in connection with these machines he managed, through the economy of his wife, to exist for about a year, during which he succeeded in reading a good many of the writers of the Scottish philosophical school.

The inevitable "bread and butter" problem, however, again presented itself. The demand for electrical energy had been dissipated by Croll's industry, and no force he could exert could conserve or create a demand which had been fairly exhausted by supply. He had to earn a livelihood for himself and wife, and what could he do? With a good deal of Micawber-like philosophy he looked for something to turn up. What did turn up would to any one but a "philosopher" have seemed a most impracticable scheme. We have it in his own words: "Some of my friends suggested that I should try a temperance hotel, and one of them stated that he was about to erect a house at Blairgowrie, and that I could have it for that purpose if I chose. After due consideration I made up my mind to try that course." There is an honest, innocent simplicity about this, which cannot fail to bring a sad smile over a business man's countenance. That a man and wife with no experience of hotel business—and very little experience of business of any kind—should start a hotel, and that a temperance hotel! Was anything more unpractical ever attempted? But that is not all. Where was this temperance hotel to be? In Blairgowrie, a village of some 3500 inhabitants, with already one hotel and fifteen public-houses or small inns in the place. Most people in such circumstances would have seen that his "friend," the builder, was looking rather to get an honest tenant for his new house than to secure a livelihood for Croll and his wife. But the impracticability of the scheme did not end there; for, as Croll says, "here was the difficulty: the house required to be furnished, and this would require a considerable sum, which I had not. It occurred to me, however, that as it would be some six or eight months before the house would be ready for occupation, and as my arm was now much improved, I might try and make a considerable number of the necessary articles before that time." Accordingly, the brave man set to work, made the most of the furniture necessary for the hotel with his own hands, and succeeded in getting the house opened in the beginning of 1852.

· As was to be expected in a small place like Blairgowrie, where there were no railways, the visitors to the temperance hotel were few and far between, and Croll and his wife were unable to make a livelihood out of the concern. He says, " Although Mrs. Croll had too much work, I, on the contrary, unfortunately had too little." With the practical wisdom of a " philosopher," he sought work in the form of endeavouring to learn Latin under the assistant teacher of the parish school. After about a year's hard labour, he acquired a knowledge of the rudiments of the language; but, finding that it would need another year to enable him to read Latin, he abandoned the thing altogether.

The temperance hotel having proved a failure after a year and a half's trial, Croll gave up the business, sold off the furniture, and left the place. He left Blairgowrie at the May term of 1853, and removed to Glasgow, where he got an engagement as an out-door canvasser for the Safety Insurance Co. This company was under the directorship of Richard Cobden, John Bright, Henry E. Gurney, Thomas Brassey, and others, whose names were a great recommendation to the company. For some time Croll was wonderfully successful as an insurance canvasser, particularly amongst the working men; but as cholera found its way to Glasgow about this date, the directors felt that it would be unwise to push the business, and consequently Croll's services were not long required. He accordingly returned again to Perth, where, through the same friend who introduced him to the tea trade, he was introduced to Dr. Robert D. Thomson, chemist, one of the directors of the Temperance Provident Institution, who was then on a visit to the city of Perth. Through him Croll was offered an agency in Dundee, and he was asked to devote his whole time to the work.

He accordingly removed to Dundee in August 1834, and began his canvassing. Here, again, he proved very successful in this uphill work. As we have already seen, Croll was very systematic in his work, and had an indomitable amount of perseverance. His method was something like this. He selected a district and sent out circulars with a prospectus containing table of rates and other information. He then called on the people to whom the circulars had been sent. Frequently he received only a cool reception from one out of thirty or forty whom he circularised and called for. When he did get this, he carefully explained the principles of insurance, the advantages of the company he represented, and tried to press the duty of insuring home to the person. Many times he had to make three or four calls on a man before he got a "proposal"; and when this was got, the sum to be insured was generally of a very limited amount. The writer has been with him on several of these canvassing visits, and could not but admire Croll's patient and persevering plan of pushing the business. His manner was quiet, earnest, and convincing. He was very serious and deliberate in the matter, he had a remarkable knowledge of the advantages of life insurance, and he readily and successfully met objections when stated. The directors of the Safety Society had not lost sight of such a serviceable man; by and by they offered him their agency in Edinburgh on much better terms than he had from the Provident in Dundee, and he at once accepted the offer. So he left Dundee in the month of May 1855, and removed to Edinburgh. He found, however, that this city was the home of insurance, and that it was much more difficult to get "proposals" there than in Dundee. Besides, the "Safety" was an English office, and although the names of the directors were a source of strength, it was a comparatively new office, and had not any exceptional advantages to offer over those of old established Scottish offices which had their chief places of business, with resident directors and local influence, in the city.

In the spring of 1856, his father, David Croll, died at the paternal home in Wolfhill, at the good old age of seventy-five, having passed the allotted span of threescore years and ten, and done an honest life's hard work.

About this time took place the failure of the Western Bank of Scotland, which threw thousands who were in comparative comfort into penury, and seriously affected commercial enterprise. Nothing so prejudicially affects insurance business as a disaster like this, and Croll as well as all other insurance agents felt this keenly. He could not prosecute insurance business to any extent in the evenings; and, accordingly, after his work during the day was finished, he utilised his spare hours in the prosecution of his favourite study, philosophy. Now he began his study of Kant, perhaps the profoundest and most original thinker of modern times, of whom he says: " With the exception of Edwards, no writer has made such an impression on my mind as Kant." No wonder that this great philosopher should produce such an impression on a purely philosophical mind; the marvel would have been had it been otherwise. The remarkable thing is that he should link with this giant of modern thought the name of Edwards. But it has to be borne in mind that it was Edwards who shone out as a sun on the darkness of his early mind, who appeared as a light at the early dawn of his philosophic life, quickened all his intellectual powers, and cleared to a large extent his pathway for future study and investigation. The persistent study of philosophy in which Croll was now engaged in his evening hours soon began to strain his eyesight seriously, and brought on an ocular affection which was accompanied by considerable pain. Since infancy he had been more or less subject to a pain at the opening of the head, which seemed now to transfer itself to the eyes. He therefore resorted to a plan of reading with the aid of a piece of plain coloured glass placed on the book; and this had the effect of mitigating the pain in the eyes. It continued, however, to afflict him not a little for several years, but he went on reading with his coloured glass despite the pain.

In 1856 the Directors of the Safety Insurance Company, finding that not much progress was being made by their office in the city of Edinburgh, thought that Croll might be tried in a more industrial centre; and, accordingly, they asked him to go to Leicester, where there was a large working-class population. One of the directors happened to be a member of Parliament for the town at the time, and it was believed that his name and influence would work a charm on intending insurers. Unfortunately, " the people of Leicester seemed to think that one of the old-established Scotch offices was fully as safe as the Safety." Notwithstanding all Croll's patience and perseverance, very few proposals could be got for the Safety; and the months spent in Leicester proved one of the hardest and most trying periods of his life.

After being about six months in Leicester, Mrs. Croll became seriously ill, and the medical men consulted recommended her to leave the place. This she did as soon as she was able to be removed, and Croll returned with her to Glasgow. There she lay ill for about a year, but, under the careful nursing of her sister and the assiduous attention of her husband, she at length recovered.

Of course, Croll could not leave his wife in her delicate state of health to go back to Leicester; and indeed there was not much inducement to return. He accordingly bade that town good-bye, and as the Safety Company had already tried Scotland with too little success to warrant their having an agent in Glasgow, he left their employment. He, however, got an engagement

6

readily from the Temperance Provident Institution, for which he had formerly done good work. Paisley was the place selected for his operations; but the "Paisley people" have always been rather difficult to deal with, and, as a shrewd observer of human nature once remarked, it is necessary "to keep your eye on Paisley." After six or eight months' trial of insurance canvassing in this old weaving town, Croll was obliged to give it up as a hopeless task; and he " then formally abandoned the insurance business altogether, after spending [in it] four and a half years of about the most disagreeable part of my life." Thus closed Croll's career as an insurance canvasser. Any one who knew the man can only marvel that he continued in it so long and proved comparatively so successful. To the ordinary observer a more unlikely man for an insurance canvasser could hardly be imagined than Croll. As he says, "To one like me, naturally so fond of retirement and even of solitude, it was painful having constantly to make up to strangers." Yet how bravely he struggled on in spite of his dislike of the work, and his constitutional inaptitude for it ! His indomitable perseverance and manly independence alone made him a fairly successful agent despite these drawbacks; and it need only be added here that he earned the respect and confidence of the directors of both institutions in which he served in this capacity, leaving the Temperance Institution to the regret of all those connected with its management.

CHAPTER V

LITERARY WORK

HAVING left Paisley, Croll returned to Glasgow in 1857, but for some time failed to obtain any remunerative employment. He could not be idle, so he commenced to bring together some thoughts on the Metaphysics of Theism. On this subject he had been thinking seriously for several years, and the following remarks by an able writer in the *Christian News* are interesting in this connection :— " We met Mr. Croll first about the year 1854 in Glasgow. He was then deeply interested in theology and philosophy. We foregathered in an old book-shop, and had long talks over the doctrine of the Will as explained by Edwards, and other kindred topics which then occupied his attention. At that time he called himself a ' moderate Calvinist,' and under that designation published a pamphlet on Predestination. It was pronounced by the Rev. Dr. Morison, no mean judge, ' an extraordinary production.' He also about that time published a pamphlet on the bearings of geology and astronomy on the creation of the world. Dr. Croll took a special interest in the doctrine of the divine existence, and his first volume of any size and pretension was *The Philosophy of Theism*. This is a thoughtful work, and displays not a little philosophical insight and acumen. It was eagerly discussed by a knot of students who used to meet with the author in the old book store. Tappan's works on the Will and Cousin's History of Philosophy were in the hands at that time of not a few who met with Dr. Croll.

The discussions and talk were always of the most friendly character,—though there were few tougher opponents than the author of *The Philosophy of Theism*. We think we see him still, calmly laying down his propositions and pressing home his arguments. If some of the more impetuous youths would break in with a word, he would listen to it, and then with outstretched hand would resume the thread of his argument and go on to the end. In these days he was highly respected, honoured, and loved, felt to be a master of philosophic thought, and the possessor of more than ordinary mental power. He was a devoted student of Hitchcock of the United States, and intended to republish his works in this country. The prospectus of his *Psychology* was issued, but the work never appeared. All the time, Dr. Croll was studying the great scientific problems which engaged the time and thought of savants. He revelled in these studies till he mastered many of them, and advanced in certain directions further than any of his contemporaries."

The Philosophy of Theism did not make its appearance so easily as is indicated by the foregoing sketch. It seems to have been rapidly composed, probably in three or four months, but it was the result of many years' hard reading and earnest thinking. At first, Croll intended merely to write a few columns on the Dependence of Theism on Metaphysics for a local newspaper. He soon found, however, that in the short space allotted for such an article, nothing like justice could be done to the subject. He therefore abandoned his original purpose, and continued writing until he had produced a volume. After it was written, he was at a loss what to do with it. He had not the means to publish it at his own cost, and publishers were chary of a work on such a peculiar subject, which must necessarily have only a limited circulation. He tried several publishers, who, though all satisfied of the merit of the work, were not prepared to run the risk of publishing a work on such a subject by an unknown author.

At last a firm agreed to take the risk of publishing on the system of "half profits" after the expenses were paid. Only five hundred copies were printed, and the book appeared anonymously. It was favourably criticised by the press, though Croll himself says it "attracted but little general attention." The subject was one, however, not calculated to attract much general attention, and it is a very high tribute to the intrinsic merit of the work that an anonymous book on an abstruse subject should have received the notice it did, and that it sold to such an extent. It not only paid all expenses, but left something over to divide as profit. What that was we have not been able to ascertain definitely, but when the publishers remitted to Croll the sum of ten pounds as a first instalment, he felt much gratified.

The aim of the work is stated in the preface as follows, "The direct object of the work is not to prove the existence of God, but to investigate the *method* to be pursued, in order to arrive at a proof of his existence.

"In the first part we have attempted to show that a purely *à priori* or a purely *à posteriori* proof of the existence of God is impossible. We cannot, on the one hand, arrive at a proof by means of *à priori* elements alone without experience; neither can we, on the other, by means of *experience*, without *à priori* elements. The only possible way, then, is by a method which combines both. We have thus two elements in the proof, objects or *facts of experience*, and *à priori principles*. But before we can legitimately use these principles in our proof, in opposition to the atheist, we must first establish their validity. This we cannot do without having recourse to metaphysics. But here a formidable difficulty meets us at the outset; for metaphysics itself is a science, the validity of which few atheists will acknowledge. And, to add to our difficulty, theists themselves have generally misunderstood or underrated this science. We are therefore necessitated to enter into a vindication of metaphysics, which forms Part II. We find that the chief objection urged against metaphysics, is the fact of its present imperfection when compared with mathematics and the natural sciences. We are then led into an examination of the essential difference between metaphysics and mathematics, in order to show that, from the very nature of metaphysics, it must succeed mathematics, and that its present imperfect state is no proof whatever of any essential defect in its nature. After this, we are prepared to enter into the third, and last, part of the work, a discussion of the method of proof. But before proceeding far, we find that we must have recourse to the principle of causality, and here, again, another difficulty meets us; for this principle is in about as unsettled a state as metaphysics itself, and we are then led into a long discussion, in order to fix precisely its nature and import; after which, all that remains is simply the exposition of the method of proof."

The Rev. Dr. Morison, of Glasgow, writes regarding this volume: "I wrote a critique upon it for the *Evangelical Repository*, December 1857. In his volume Dr. Croll says: 'I affirm that it is an absolute impossibility, a thing which never was, is, or can be, namely, that the will should determine its own acts.'

"I on my part affirmed and still affirm that the will is self-determining. Dr. Croll held by Jonathan Edwards. I on my part held more by Tappan than Edwards. My criticism was severe, but it did not break the friendship that subsisted between us, and which, I am happy to say, continued unabated to the close of his life. The longer I knew Dr. Croll, the more I admired him." The truth of the foregoing observation regarding the severity of the criticism not disturbing their friendly relations is well illustrated by the following letter:—

21 NEW SNEDDON STREET, PAISLEY,
29th October 1857.

REV. JAMES MORISON—DEAR SIR,—Referring to *The Philosophy of Theism*, it would have led to a better understanding in regard to its arrangement, had I stated that the direct object of the work is the solution of the following problem. Given an organic body, show how it can be *rationally* proved that its cause *must* have been a personality, endowed with intelligence, will, and sensitivity,—that the entire argument is contained in Part III. Sections 1, 2, 3, 9, 10, 11, 12, 13, 14; and that the rest of the book was written, either in anticipation of objections, or to pave the way to the argument. I shall feel obliged if you will, at your leisure, read these sections by themselves in the order I have marked them.

I am, etc., JAMES CROLL.

The following letters from Professor Ferrier and Principal Cairns may also be quoted as indicating the opinions of the merits of the work formed by two distinguished thinkers belonging to different philosophical schools :—

ST. ANDREWS, 15*th January* 1859.

DEAR SIR,—I have read attentively the volume entitled *The Philosophy of Theism*, and I am impressed with the acuteness and power of coherent and independent thought which it displays. The style is concise and, for those who are at all conversant with the subjects treated of, perspicuous. The main object of the treatise, to show mainly the distinction between will as producing, and intelligence as determining motion, is well made out. In some form or other this distinction is essential to the Theistic argument; and I am not aware of any quarter where it is more clearly stated than it is in this book. There are many other topics touched upon in the volume in a way which shows a thoughtful and original consideration of the subject: and I believe that all who are interested in philosophical inquiries may read it with profit and satisfaction. Even where they may not agree with it, the book will assist in rendering their own ideas more definite and clear.—Yours faithfully, J. F. FERRIER.

MR. JAMES CROLL.

BERWICK, 12*th August* 1858.

GENTLEMEN,—About a year ago you sent me a treatise on *The Philosophy of Theism*, and afterwards wrote requesting my opinion of it. I was obliged altogether to decline a judgment, as my health was very much broken, and I was not equal to my necessary duties. I have since so far recovered as to study a little, and having read the work with some care, though still without critical accuracy, I venture to express my sense of its qualities.

I am much pleased with the advanced state of intelligence displayed by the writer as to the exact shape and pressure of metaphysical questions at the present time. He has evidently read in many schools; and, what is still better, he is a vigorous and independent thinker, who can grasp the essence of a subject, and express it without either vagueness or pedantic nicety in clear and comprehensible English.

His work is a positive contribution to the theistic argument, and I regard him as on the right track, for the argument from causality, however decried by some, is the only valid basis of philosophical theism, and there is both ingenuity and solidity in the way he connects the causal principle with the design argument, so as to reason from the determinations of motion that make up organised bodies. I think, however, that this trunk line of his argument needs to be made a little more prominent, and regret, though his digressions are both able and satisfactory, that they somewhat hide the main thread of discussion. Nor, so far as I remember, admitting as he does that the ordinary argument for the contingency of the universe is invalid, has he supplied any other proof of the non-eternity of matter with its present dispositions and arrangements, so as to make way for the causal principle and its consequences, as he holds it.

I am much interested by the intelligence and vigour of his reduction of all science to metaphysical starting-points, and also by the vindication of free will as an ontological question from falling under the testimony of consciousness. This is one of the most original things in the book, and betokens a strong thinker. His frequent references to Kant, so far as I remember, are accurate; only I think that Kant and he mean the same thing respecting mathematical reasoning as founded on sensuous imaginations. Kant does not mean that this is *à priori* in the same sense as the categories of the understanding, though he uses the word; and the writer does not mean, by calling it "empirical," that it could ever be based on mere observation, without the antecedent intuitions of space which make observation possible, and which, according to Kant, account for, by necessitating, the harmony between *à priori* or abstract mathematical truths and the actual world of lines and figures.

But I do not go into further details. I regard the work as one of no ordinary promise, far above the great body of similar contributions. The writer, I hope, will produce something still better, and needs only to give himself entirely to this topic or any other to secure distinguished success.

Again thanking you for sending me the work, and apologising for my long delay,—I am, etc.

JOHN CAIRNS.

It is a remarkable testimony to the candour and critical ability of Dr. Cairns that he should, from the perusal of this anonymous volume, predict that the writer needed only to give himself entirely to this topic or any other to achieve distinguished success. This expression of prophetic insight was wonderfully verified in Croll's case, who afterwards achieved such distinguished success, writing on very different topics.

Croll had forwarded a copy of *The Philosophy of Theism* to the late Principal Barclay of Glasgow University, from whom he received the following letter:—

CURRIE, *6th May*, 1858.

SIR,—I beg to apologise for having delayed so long to thank you for presenting me with a copy of *The Philosophy of Theism*. It furnishes very satisfactory evidence that you have thought deeply on what must be admitted to be a deep subject.

I very much sympathise with you in your desire to have the benefit of a university education, and if my influence can avail in obtaining a bursary for you, it shall be most willingly used.—I am, dear sir, yours faithfully,

T. BARCLAY.

JAMES CROLL, ESQ.

This shows how anxious Croll was to have the benefit of a thorough systematic university education, a desire which he was destined never to be able to have satisfied. The book, however, had evidently secured the kindly interest and sympathy of the learned Principal, who, as will be afterwards seen, when opportunity offered, did not hesitate to use his influence in furthering Croll's interests.

The Philosophy of Theism, although it did not attract much general attention, established conclusively the fact that the writer was a man of considerable mental power, who could express his thoughts in clear, forcible style. The reputation thus gained led to his appointment on the *Commonwealth*, a weekly newspaper published in Glasgow, and chiefly devoted to the promotion of the temperance cause. As Croll was an ardent abstainer, this was a sphere in which he could, and did, work with a will.

In the spring of 1858 his mother, Janet Croll, died in the old house at Wolfhill, at the advanced age of seventy-seven. His brother David, who, as already mentioned, was somewhat deformed, having now no one to look after the home, left Wolfhill and went to reside with Croll in Glasgow.

About the middle of the year 1858, Croll met with an accident which caused considerable pain and discomfort, as well as unfitted him in the future for much physical exertion. He says: "One day, while suddenly exerting my whole strength in using a joiner's plane in dressing a piece of wood, something appeared to give way about the region of the heart. Medical men have never been able to detect what is wrong, But ever since then, though my health and strength remained unimpaired, I dared not lift anything, or attempt to run or even walk fast."

Notwithstanding this, he continued his duties in the *Commonwealth* office. He remained in this situation for about a year and a half. About the end of that period, the directors of the Andersonian College, Glasgow, advertised for a janitor, and Croll applied for the situation. It appears that during his stay in Glasgow Croll had spent some time at Thornliebank, where Walter Crum, Esq., the Chairman of the Andersonian, lived. This gentleman had casually come across Croll there, and learned to respect him. Through his influence, aided, it is said, by that of Professor Ferrier of St. Andrews and Principal Barclay of Glasgow, Croll was appointed to the humble post. He entered on his new duties at the end of the autumn of 1859, and, within the walls of the Andersonian, found a quiet resting-place for several years. "Taking it all in all," he says, " I have not been in any place so congenial to me as that institution proved. After upwards of twenty years of an unsettled life, full of hardships and difficulties, it was a relief to get settled down in what might be regarded as a permanent home. My salary was small, it is true, little more than sufficient to enable us to subsist, but this was compensated by advantages for me of another kind."

His duties in this institution were of a somewhat humble nature; but they did not tax his mental powers, so that in leisure hours he was fresh for such intellectual work as he found congenial. "The Museum was open from 11 A.M. till 3 P.M., and as I had little or nothing to do with the arranging and classification of the specimens, and there were but few visitors, I had generally a few hours a day of a quiet time for reading and study." His brother David was of great assistance to him in the performance of his duties. In fact, he superintended and performed most of the routine and mechanical work of seeing the rooms cleaned, the fires kept up, and the doors opened and class-rooms aired.

A student of the time writes: "The first time I saw Mr. Croll would be as he stood at the door of the foot of the stair leading to the lecture hall in which the lectures to the evening classes were delivered, as I showed him my ticket as a passport for entrance. I mind that he never officiously demanded a sight of it, but simply gave it a glance when shown to him. Croll was very obliging. When a student wanted to hear any single lecture to which he had not a class ticket, he readily admitted him with a nod. This showed his strong sympathy with any real student thirsting for knowledge. Only to a known student of the institution, however, was the privilege accorded, and that only for 'any single lecture,' so that the teacher really suffered nothing, while the anxious inquirer might profit much."

Croll had evening as well as day duties to perform; but the most irksome and disagreeable duty was that of collecting subscriptions from private gentlemen for the support of the institution. This was odious to Croll, perhaps even more so than insurance canvassing, as he was often met with the remark that if his university could not support itself, it should be given up. Yet not a word of murmur escaped his lips, and the subject is not even referred to in his Autobiography.

During his period of janitorship he had access to the fine scientific library belonging to the Glasgow Philosophical Society, a privilege of which he availed himself. "Here also was the library of four or five thousand volumes in connection with the evening classes of the institution, and, further, the private library of the founder of the institution, consisting of over two thousand volumes."

The attractions of these libraries, containing a large number of the most valuable works on physical science, were so great as to draw off his attention to a considerable extent from his philosophical and theological studies, and for a time he resolved to devote his attention entirely to the prosecution of that department of study. Accordingly, he resumed the study of physics at the place where he had left off in former years.

It will be remembered that when Croll was only about fifteen or sixteen years of age, he studied " the laws of motion and the fundamental principles of mechanics. In like manner I studied pneumatics, hydrostatics, light, heat, electricity, and magnetism," without any assistance, as there was no one near him who could really help him. These were the subjects of which he resumed the investigation now, in the congenial atmosphere of the Andersonian Institution. As in earlier years he had never burdened his memory with the mere details of the physical sciences, but pressed on till he had grasped " the laws or principles which they were intended to illustrate," so he still pursued the same plan. Croll could never keep the results of his study bottled up in his brain for his own selfish satisfaction, but was always, from his earliest down to his latest days, ready and anxious to let others have the benefit of his investigations. So now, no sooner had he made any discovery than he longed to communicate it for the general benefit. He thought very little of the monetary reward he might receive for his scientific work, although he never enjoyed much of this world's wealth. Many important papers were gratuitously sent by him to various magazines, and even when he did receive fees for his articles, they were frequently spent in reprinting separate copies to be sent to scholars at home and abroad. We may truly say that a more unselfish, a more generous man of science, a man more wholly free from the "odium scientificum" than James Croll never breathed.

Dr. Morison writes, regarding Dr. Croll, under date

3rd September 1891 : " My acquaintance with Dr. Croll commenced very soon after my removal to Glasgow in 1851. In these early days I had a large and lively theological class. The subjects discussed thrilled into the souls of not a few noble youths ; and, indeed, the influence of the class exercises continues, in a subtle form, to the present day, strong and sweet.

" Dr. Croll found his way into this class not exactly as a member, for he put no questions, but as an interested spectator and listener.

" We soon came to know each other, and thenceforward our intercourse grew apace, for I was able to assist him somewhat in literary work. It was not that our thoughts ran in absolute unison. They did not. But somehow we loved one another with pure hearts fervently. Our intimacy increased as time rolled on, and I not infrequently found myself turning into his little room in the ' Andersonian,' that we might exercise a little fencing on some of our favourite battlefields. Dr. Croll about that period revelled among the new books that were laid, as it were, to his hand in the ' University.'

" He had obtained a humble position as bedellus of that vigorous educational institute. He diligently improved his opportunity, and struck on many new veins of ideas which led him far and wide into the interminable fields of science, pure and simple. He had been from early life an omnivorous reader. But the new views of science soon received from him the lion's share of his attention—the place of pre-eminence as regards his most thoughtful thinking on the one hand, and his miscellaneous reading on the other.

" Ere long the consciousness of latent power grew within him, and continued to grow, till an overmastering conviction came upon him, to the effect that he too, as well as others, had a service laid upon him in the way of guiding some of the chief scientific currents of the age. With a view to fulfil this mission, he read and wrote largely on Molecular Physics. It was his first great effort, the beginning and inauguration of a bright scientific career. Even as regards style of composition he reached maturity by leaps and bounds. The style in which he settled was conspicuous for dignity, manliness, and for translucency."

CHAPTER VI

EARLY SCIENTIFIC WORK

HAVING settled down quietly in the humble sphere of janitor of the Andersonian University in 1859, where the duties, not of a laborious though mostly menial kind, were largely performed by his brother, Croll found the College a congenial home, as he resided on the premises. To most men of mental ability the situation would probably have been monotonous and irksome; but Croll, with his contented disposition and studious habits, found himself planted in a comparatively congenial sphere. For fifteen years previous to his going there, he had been engaged in philosophical and theological studies; and he had already put the result of some of these studies into systematic form. He found the attractions of physical science and the facilities afforded for its study in the Andersonian Library too strong to resist; and, accordingly, he threw himself with characteristic vigour into that department.

From 1859 to 1864 there is really little or nothing to record regarding his personal life, as the due performance of his daily duties at the University, and the equally steady amount of daily scientific study, occupied him from week to week and year to year with little variety. He was fond of long walks in the country, and was a keen observer and admirer of the beauties of nature. His daily walks were most frequently taken alone, so that what he observed might be noted down either on the spot or immediately when he returned home. He was essentially a solitary student and observer of nature, and did not care for his mental meditations being disturbed by ordinary conversation. It will be remembered that even during his boyhood he had studied physical science with considerable success, and that in those early studies his inclination was more to the mastery of first principles than scientific details. So likewise now, when the opportunity was afforded him of access to the best scientific works in the Andersonian Library, the bent of his mind led him to the study of first principles. Having ascertained these on a given branch of science, his object in all his studies was to advance that science either by the further application of the principles known, or more generally by the investigation and discovery of some new principle. Hence all the results of his observation, investigation, and study, so soon as put into shape, were speedily communicated to the scientific and reading public, both through the medium of scientific societies and the press. With characteristic courtesy and kindly consideration, he was always ready to give any scientific man the benefit of his studies, and to spare no pains in communicating the results thereof, as will be seen later on.

In the subsequent part of this book it is proposed to incorporate the gist of the numerous papers contributed by Dr. Croll to various learned societies and publications. A complete list of these works, with references to the sources where they may be found, is printed in an appendix; and the numbers used in the following account of them correspond to these in that list.

In the early years of his scientific labours, Mr. Croll published several very interesting contributions, which showed that he was busily occupied in thinking out for himself some of the great problems that were being ardently discussed by the leading physicists in the sixties. During the whole of his life he continued to interest himself in his early studies, and occasionally published a paper bearing on physical problems; but for many years he devoted his attention chiefly to the great problems of theoretic geology, and, in 1864, he began the brilliant series of solutions which make his name one of the most illustrious in the history of this science. In 1865 he discussed, in the now defunct *Reader*, the physical cause of the submergence of the land during the Glacial epoch, and pointed out that the North Sea must have been invaded by land ice during that period.

From that time onwards he produced in quick succession a series of papers of the greatest importance, in which he dealt with the secular variations of climate, more particularly during the Glacial period, and gradually developed his theories of their cause. In ten years' time he had so far elaborated and arranged his results that he could publish *Climate and Time*, a book that was at once recognised as an epoch-making work on theoretic geology. A summary of this work, after four years' further reflection, was published in the *Encyclopædia Britannica* (Article " Geology "), and also in Sir Archibald Geikie's *Text-Book of Geology*. Occasional physical papers had appeared during the ten years devoted to *Climate and Time*; but after its publication they became more frequent. All had some connection with the ideas that had occupied his attention so long and so profitably, and deal with such subjects as the Origin and Age of the Sun, Nebulæ, etc.

Mr. Croll's papers are distinguished by remarkable concentration of thought, joined to a very great lucidity of exposition. They are, therefore, not less interesting and intelligible to the general reader than valuable to the special student.

In order to make the account of Dr. Croll's scientific work as brief and clear as possible, the papers have been considered in six groups, within each of which a chronological order has, as far as possible, been followed :—

1. Early Physical Papers, 1861–1864.
2. Age and Origin of the Sun. Nebulæ.
3. Geological Climate and Chronology.

4. Glacial Epoch and Glaciers.
5. Ocean Currents.
6. Miscellaneous Papers.

The most weighty contributions are those summarised in Nos. 3, 4, and 5.

1. EARLY PHYSICAL PAPERS, 1861–1864.

Croll was a man who never went into anything without adequate preparation, or adopted theories without making the most thorough investigation possible and applying the most rigid tests that could be devised. Accordingly, before he wrote on any subject, he took all the precautions which his mind could suggest to verify any propositions he might advance. Thus we find that, before he began writing on Physics at all, he went through a course of reading, which to a trained student would be considered tolerably hard work, but which to Croll, with his weak eyesight and other defects, must have been a prolonged mental effort. During the years 1860 and 1861 he appears to have chiefly occupied himself with the study and investigation of the results of the researches of Faraday, Joule, Thomson, Tyndall, Rankine, and others on Heat, Electricity, and Magnetism. The immediate result of these studies was the publication of his paper in 1861 on Ampère's experiment. It appeared in the *Philosophical Magazine* in the month of April of that year, and was entitled " Remarks on Ampère's Experiment on the Repulsion of a Rectilinear Electrical Current on itself" (No. 2).

In May 1862 he returned to the same subject, and wrote another paper entitled " Remarks on Ampère's Experiment on the Repulsion of a Rectilinear Current on itself" (No. 4), which appeared in the *Philosophical Magazine* of that month. In October 1862 he wrote an explanatory note on " Ampèrian Repulsion " (No. 7), accompanied by an illustrated figure, which appeared in the *Philosophical Magazine* of that year.

These communications by Croll throw much light on the extent and depth of his knowledge of electricity. Forty years previously, Ampère had discovered the peculiar action of one current of electricity on another, and also the laws which regulate such action. He found, for example, that if two hoops are hung up beside one another with their planes vertical, and so attached to their supports as to be capable of rotating round a vertical axis, and a current of electricity then passed through each, the two hoops will rotate until they are parallel to one another, the electric current flowing in the same direction in both.

From this Ampère proceeded to examine what action, if any, a current has upon itself. He bent a piece of wire into the shape of an elongated U, and then bent the curved part so as to be in a plane at right angles to that of the straight parallel portions. The wire thus bent was laid upon mercury contained in two separate parallel channels, so that one of the straight parts floated on the mercury in each channel. In this way the straight portions of the wire could move endways with great freedom, while always connected together at one end by the curved part, which formed an arch between them. When the two portions of mercury were connected with the terminals of a battery, a current passed from one to the other by way of the floating wire, and it was found that, under these circumstances, the wire always moved away from the ends of channels with which the battery was connected. This experiment led Ampère to believe that a current was self-repellent; and his experiment was held as establishing this astonishing fact for many years.

In 1861, Principal Forbes, of St. Andrews University, read a paper before the Royal Society of Edinburgh, in which he described an experiment seemingly at variance with the self-repellent theory. His experiment was similar to Ampère's in theory, with the exception that the movable bend of the circuit was detached from the rest; and he found that this movable joint not only was not repelled, but was held strongly attached to the fixed part of the circuit. He also threw doubt on the experiment of Ampère ever having been successfully performed, or at least verified up till then.

A paper of Croll's appeared in the *Philosophical Magazine* (No. 2) at this time, showing, with considerable subtlety, that, although Ampère's experiment were successful, it would not prove that a current repelled itself, as the experiment could otherwise be easily explained. He showed, in addition, how this theory led to manifest contradictions. He was therefore led to adopt the theory propounded by Principal Forbes, although here again he showed that the attraction of the movable bend could be explained without assuming that the attraction was caused by the moving current. Here the matter rested until Maxwell showed that the experiment gives no proof of what force any one portion of a current exerts upon another.

In March 1862, Croll read a paper before the Chemical Society of Glasgow on "The Relation of Chemical Combination to Specific Heat" (No. 3), in which he showed that by applying heat to solids or liquids, part of it raises the temperature and part works against mechanical cohesion, the relative proportions of each being according to their relative resistance; and that, therefore, the specific heat of bodies increases as the temperature rises. The general principle is, that, other things being equal, the more easily fused a body is, the greater its specific heat.

To the meeting of the British Association in 1862 Mr. Croll communicated a paper on "The Cohesion of Gases, and its Relation to Recent Experiments on the Thermal Effects of Elastic Fluids in Motion" (No. 5).

In this paper, he points out that the deviations from Boyle's law, seen in such easily liquefiable gases as carbonic acid gas, can readily be explained by the cohesion of their particles. He also holds that cohesion explains why, in gases which deviate most from Boyle's law, the co-efficient of expansion is greatest, the co-efficient of expansion increases with the density, and, when compressed under the same conditions, most work is done, and when expanded by heat, least work is done.

Cohesion and Thomson and Joule's Experiments on the Thermal Effect of Elastic Fluids in Motion.—In these experiments of Thomson and Joule, gases which had been highly compressed in a vessel were allowed to escape through a porous plug, and were then found to have a lower temperature than when they were compressed. As the cooling due to the expansion of the gas is not compensated for by the heat of friction, Croll suggested that part of the heat must have been used in overcoming the cohesion of the gas. He could not suggest an explanation if, as is said, the temperature of the expanded gas is, in some cases, highest.

Cohesion and Carnot's Function.—Dr. Joule suggested this formula for Carnot's function: $\mu = \dfrac{J\,E}{1 + E\,T}$ where J = Joule's equivalent, E = co-efficient of expansion, and T = temperature in degrees centigrade. Professor Thomson noted that this does not always give the true value. As the temperature of a gas diminishes, the amount of heat consumed by cohesion increases. But with saturated vapours the reverse holds good, cohesion increases as the temperature rises. Only for a perfect gas can the formula hold at all temperatures. For imperfect gases and vapours the function will deviate in opposite directions.

At this time the great question discussed by physicists was the dynamical theory of heat, and Croll made several contributions to the controversy. In his paper, "On the Mechanical Power of Electro-Magnetism," communicated to the British Association in 1862 (No. 6), he contends that, when a current is reduced from A to B, although the heat evolved in the conducting wire is now x B^2 instead of A^2, the heat in the entire circuit is really B, the missing heat being found in the battery. If mechanical work be done, the heat given off in the whole circuit, from the same current, will be diminished by the thermal equivalent of the work performed, which he shows to be derived from the electric current. This he explains by supposing the molecules to have resistance, so that when the one at the pole of the battery is set in motion by chemical action, this disturbs the next particle, and so on, giving the series of molecular vibrations which we perceive as heat. In the electro-magnetic machine the current generated by chemical action passing through soft iron makes the molecules magnetic, and equilibrium is regained by the mechanical work done. This will be greater as the resistance producing heat is diminished, and it also depends on the " amount of resistance offered by the magnetic element as an outlet to the electric force"; so that the harder the iron, the less the mechanical work. Hence the amount of molecular resistance determines the amount of molecular work producing heat, or mechanical work produced by electro-magnetism.

Croll next compared *chemical and vital forces and their relations to the potential energies of matter*, in a paper on " The Relation of Chemical Affinity to Vital Force," published in the *Chemical News* on 16th May 1863 (No. 8). Chemical change turns potential into kinetic energy; but heat cannot bring back the former condition, nor can electric currents, for more potential energy is lost in generating the current than is gained in electrolysis. But vital agencies seem to separate atoms of strong affinities, restoring potential energies from actual energy of the sun's rays. Thus, as he shows, " the chemical agent restores the potential energy by consuming actual energy, viz. the sun's rays."

In 1864, Croll wrote three papers dealing with the theory of heat, the first (No. 9) being a short reply to some objections raised by Mr. Gill to the dynamical theory. In the second, on " The Nature of Heat Vibrations" (No. 1), he explained these as molecular and not molar, and concluded that the ultimate atom was necessarily elastic, the heat-vibrations consisting of alternate expansions and contractions of the atom itself.

The last paper, on "The Cause of the Cooling Effect produced on Solids by Tension (No. 12), may be summarised in his own words: "Previous to the application of tension, the heat existing in the molecules is unable to produce any expansion against the force of cohesion. But when the influence of cohesion is partly counteracted by the tension applied, the heat becomes enabled to perform work of expansion, and a cooling effect is the result."

One of the first distinguished scientists who encouraged Croll in his studies was the late Professor Tyndall. Early in 1863, Croll had written to him regarding his physical investigations, to which the Professor replied: "Your letter was interesting to me as an illustration of power to seize a definite physical image—the molecules acting as hammers was capital. I have no doubt that anything you send me will interest me." Taking advantage of this kind note, Croll sent him the paper on "Supposed Objections to the Dynamical Theory of Heat," regarding which Professor Tyndall writes: "10th Feb. 1864.—Dear Sir,—I have forwarded your paper to Mr. Francis, altering nothing therein." Croll later on sent the Professor a further paper, and received the following reply:—

14th January 1865.

MY DEAR SIR,—It is both amusing and interesting to me to trace the parallelism which has run between your thoughts and mine on the subject of "negative fluorescence" (I have changed this term to *Calorescence*). The very experiment to which you refer, of rendering a body hot by concussion, is the one which most influenced my conviction that it was possible to produce incandescence by invisible rays.

It strikes me you are rather hard on the phrase "breaking up long periods into short ones." In the case of the hammer there is a conversion of the mechanical motion into molecular motion, and in the case of the hydrogen flame there seems to me to be a conversion of the long periods into short ones. The fact, at all events, is that you hit the mass with waves of slow recurrence, and that you obtain, in return, from the mass, waves of quick recurrence.

Excuse the hurried scrawl.

Do you wish me to send your note to the *Philosophical Magazine*? If so, I would suggest one small and unimportant alteration. Instead of saying " an abuse of language," I would say an incorrect use of language. —Yours very truly,   JOHN TYNDALL.

2. AGE AND ORIGIN OF THE SUN. NEBULÆ

In all questions of geological chronology the age of the sun is of prime importance. The heat of the sun cannot be derived from combustion, which is quite inadequate to account for it. If the sun had contracted from a nebulous mass extending far beyond the limits of the present solar system into its present size, Professor von Helmholtz had calculated that sufficient heat would be generated for twenty million years. But Croll said that geologists demanded a longer period than this to account for the earth's development, and that biologists asserted that hundreds of millions of years were needed for the evolution of the present flora and fauna. Croll considered the present rate of denudation, and deduced from data obtained in the Mississippi valley and in Europe, that the oldest sedimentary rocks are probably about 90 million years old. If this be so, some source of heat other than mere contraction of a nebular mass must be found, so that the sun may have given out heat for such a long period. Croll stated that 50 million years' heat might arise from the collision of two bodies, each half the mass of the sun, and moving at a speed of 476 miles per second before the collision. Only 274 miles per second of this speed would be accounted for by the mutual attraction of the two masses, and the rest must be assumed as due to the proper motion of the bodies. Were this original speed to be greater, a greater amount of heat would be generated. How the initial velocity was acquired cannot be explained. Supposing each sun thus formed to last 100 million years, and that all the stars visible to the naked eye were such suns, a star visible in our hemisphere would be formed only once in 15,000 years, if the number of fixed stars be constant; and so the absence of a historical record is not an argument against the theory. The permanent stars, too, are those whose translation motion has been transformed in a large measure into heat. If only a part of this motion were transformed into heat, the probabilities are that only a temporarily visible star would be formed. Supposing that a hundred such temporary stars were formed for one permanent one, and that each on an average was visible for a thousand years, only about six such stars would be visible at present, and it might well be that their greater velocity has not yet been detected.

Croll urged (Paper 71) that the nebulæ could also be explained as a stage in solar evolution. Mr. Lockyer's plausible theory of the evolution of the planets assumes a temperature far too high to be the result of condensation. This temperature cannot have been derived from gravitation, and the collision of two bodies must be the source from which it is derived. After the collision of two bodies moving with a great velocity in space, there would be an enormous mass of incandescent matter spread over a very wide area; and the known irregularity of nebulæ would be accounted for by the chance irregularity of this dispersion. Star clusters would result from this widespread and irregular distribution through space, condensation taking place round subordinate centres. In reply to objectors, Croll urged that it was perfectly legitimate to assume the existence of non-luminous bodies in space, some of which have not yet received their light and heat, and others which have spent them. The assumed velocity is quite a plausible one; and, if it has not been measured, that can be explained by the fact that on this hypothesis the visible stars are bodies whose motion in space has in great measure been transformed into heat and light. In the case when only part of the motion had been transformed, Croll pointed out that the proper motion of the fixed stars was not accurately known. Collisions, however, must be extremely rare events.

www.ingramcontent.com/pod-product-compliance
Lightning Source LLC
LaVergne TN
LVHW081347060426
835508LV00017B/1456